WITLEY CO

The Story of a Victorian Palace

By John Richard Hodges

John Richard Hodges (signature)

'Out of Monuments, Names, Words, Proverbs, Traditions, Private Records and Evidences, Fragments of Stories, Passages of Works, and the like, we do save and recover somewhat from the deluge of Time.' ~ Bacon's Advancement of Learning.

Jerusalem (1804) – William Blake

And did those feet in ancient time

Walk upon England's mountains green

And was the holy Lamb of God

On England's pleasant pastures seen

And did the Countenance Divine

Shine forth upon our clouded hills

And was Jerusalem builded here

Among these dark Satanic Mills

Bring me my Bow of burning gold

Bring me my Arrows of desire:

Bring me my Spear: O clouds unfold

Bring me my Chariot of fire.

I will not cease from Mental Fight,

Nor shall my sword sleep in my hand

Till we have built Jerusalem

In England's green and pleasant land.

For Nick-A remarkable young man- 1979-1998

There are many people

Who come and go in our lives,

a few touch us in ways

that change us forever.

You have made a difference

in my life and I am grateful.

John Richard Hodges – 2012

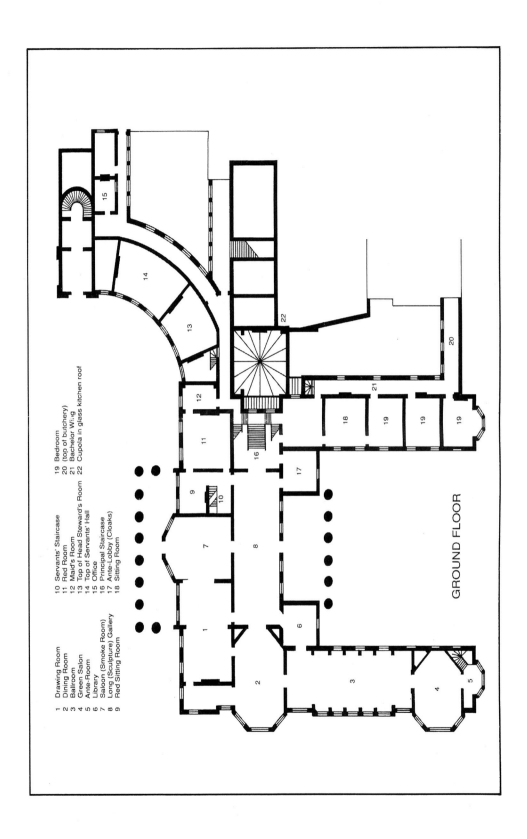

1 Drawing Room
2 Dining Room
3 Ballroom
4 Green Salon
5 Ante-Room
6 Library
7 Saloon (Smoke Room)
8 Long (Sculpture) Gallery
9 Red Sitting Room

10 Servants' Staircase
11 Red Room
12 Maid's Room
13 Top of Head Steward's Room
14 Top of Servants' Hall
15 Office
16 Principal Staircase
17 Ante-Lobby (Cloaks)
18 Sitting Room

19 Bedroom
20 (top of butchery)
21 Bachelor Wing
22 Cupola in glass kitchen roof

GROUND FLOOR

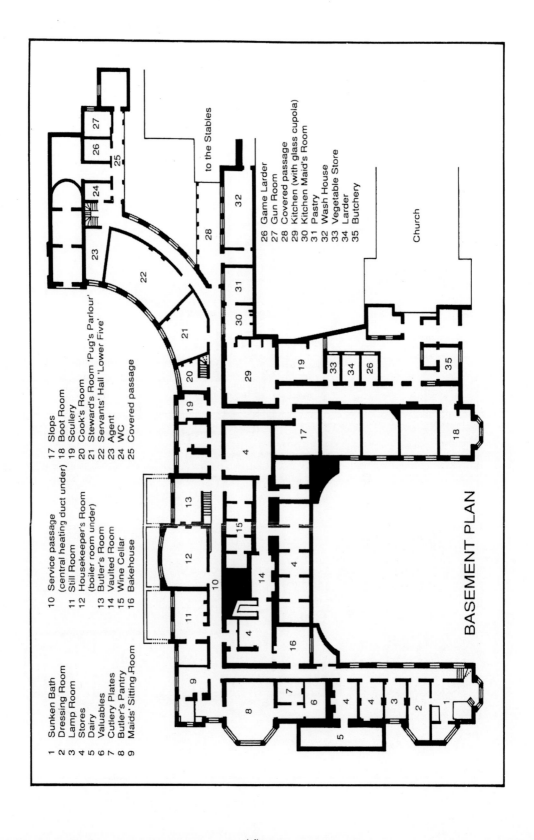

1 Sunken Bath
2 Dressing Room
3 Lamp Room
4 Stores
5 Dairy
6 Valuables
7 Cutlery Plates
8 Butler's Pantry
9 Maids' Sitting Room

10 Service passage
   (central heating duct under)
11 Still Room
12 Housekeeper's Room
   (boiler room under)
13 Butler's Room
14 Vaulted Room
15 Wine Cellar
16 Bakehouse

17 Slops
18 Boot Room
19 Scullery
20 Cook's Room
21 Steward's Room 'Pug's Parlour'
22 Servants' Hall 'Lower Five'
23 Agent
24 WC
25 Covered passage

26 Game Larder
27 Gun Room
28 Covered passage
29 Kitchen (with glass cupola)
30 Kitchen Maid's Room
31 Pastry
32 Wash House
33 Vegetable Store
34 Larder
35 Butchery

to the Stables

Church

BASEMENT PLAN

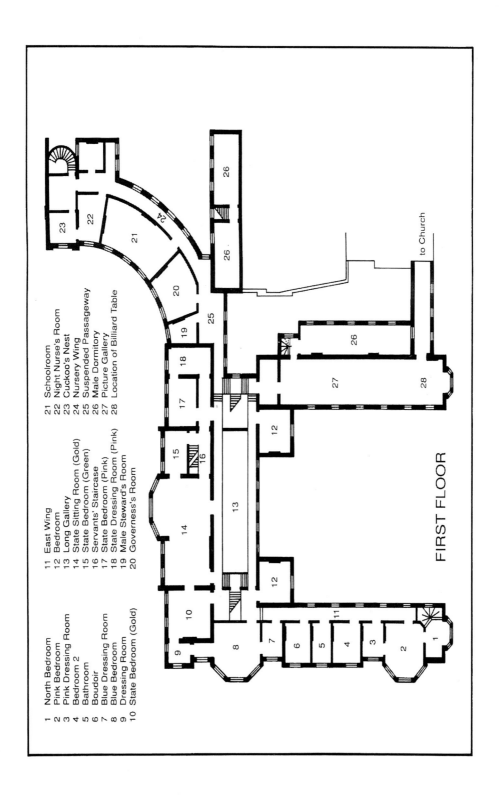

1 North Bedroom
2 Pink Bedroom
3 Pink Dressing Room
4 Bedroom 2
5 Bathroom
6 Boudoir
7 Blue Dressing Room
8 Blue Bedroom
9 Dressing Room
10 State Bedroom (Gold)

11 East Wing
12 Bedroom
13 Long Gallery
14 State Sitting Room (Gold)
15 State Bedroom (Green)
16 Servants' Staircase
17 State Bedroom (Pink)
18 State Dressing Room (Pink)
19 Male Steward's Room
20 Governess's Room

21 Schoolroom
22 Night Nurse's Room
23 Cuckoo's Nest
24 Nursery Wing
25 Suspended Passageway
26 Male Dormitory
27 Picture Gallery
28 Location of Billiard Table

to Church

FIRST FLOOR

Contents:

PREFACE:

Witley Court and the Dudley Era – c.1837-1920

In 1837 just a year after the accession of the young Queen Victoria to the throne of England and her rule over her vast Empire, the Foleys sold Witley Court and estate to William Humble Ward, who was heir to the vast industrial fortunes of the Dudleys.

From the 1740s the Dudleys had been in the forefront of the Industrial Revolution which was rapidly changing the face of England and gradually the world. Their 'Black Country' interests included ironworks, coal mines and limestone quarries. From 1837, their vast wealth enabled them to purchase a large country estate and mansion and transform this into one of the most magnificent private houses in Europe. It was visited by many crowned heads and became a byword for elegance, extravagance and luxury on an incredible scale.

An interesting 'back to front-reflection' image of the Court:- courtesy of Olive and Bernard Poultney©

Foreword – by Spencer Trickett

For many, Witley Court is a romantic ruin that captures the imagination and evokes a feeling of loss on the grand scale. Today, the skeleton frame of this once palatial residence stands alone in the Worcestershire countryside as a reminder of opulent living and wealth.

I remember my first visit to Witley Court, it was a bleak March morning and I was certain I had come the wrong way. Turning off the main road, an uneven dirt track lead me through the trees and eventually to the imposing North Portico. Before getting out of the car, I sat for a while in awe at the majestic sight in front of me. How could a building of this size be so derelict? I took my time exploring the ruin; I was the only visitor there and was able to soak up the atmosphere of the decaying building. There were weeds and trees growing within the building and the south parterre did not resemble a formal garden, the house felt unloved and forgotten. Reminders of the elegance were punctuated around the ruin, decorative plasterwork, and elaborate iron steps, beautifully hand carved stone work, and marble flooring and the fabulous fountains were all on show and still capturing the visitor's attention.

After my first visit, I left Witley Court feeling quite drained and saddened by what I had witnessed. Like so many before me, I was falling in love with a building. Within months I had managed to get a job there. When I started there were no paths, steps, flower beds, carriage drive way or working fountain. There wasn't even a proper admission point- just a small wooden hut in front of the house. How lucky we are to this is not now the case. The balance of a ruined stately home and the restored formal garden work perfectly.

For 14 years, Witley Court became my second home. Seasons were shared and visitors came and went and came back again! Every moment I spent amongst the ruins were months of pure fascination and delight. I could see, for many, this was the same case.

John was certainly one of those visitors who had been bitten by the Witley bug. I was delighted to hear that he is planning to write a book on Witley Court, especially as there are very few 'Witley Fans' to own! John is a gentleman with a genuine passion to learn about the past, present and future of Witley Court. This book is a doorway into the past at Witley and is a must for all who have connected with this grand listed building. For those who have explored, imagined, picnicked and been intrigued to find out more about Witley, then this is the book for you.

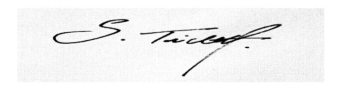

Spencer Trickett – October 2012

Witley Court- Timeline:

- ➢ *Foley Years:*
- ➢ *1ˢᵗ Earl Dudley- (27ᵗʰ March 1817-7ᵗʰ May 1885) – came into his inheritance*
- ➢ *1835 – Attended both Christ Church and Trinity College in Oxford*
- ➢ *1837-Purchased Witley Court Estate (16 years of age) for an estimated £680,000 (c.£40,800,000).*
- ➢ *Queen Adelaide rented Witley Court from 1843-46.*
- ➢ *1ˢᵗ Marriage to Selina Constance De Burgh on 24ᵗʰ April 1851.*
- ➢ *Created Earl of Dudley (2ⁿᵈ creation) and Viscount Ednam on February 13ᵗʰ 1860.*
- ➢ *2ⁿᵈ Marriage to Georgina Elizabeth Moncrieffe (30 years age difference) on November 21ˢᵗ 1865.*
- ➢ *Died on the 7ᵗʰ May 1885 (68 years of age). Buried at Witley Church but later in 1953 reburied in Worcester Cathedral.*
- ➢ *2ⁿᵈ Earl Dudley- (1867-1932).*
- ➢ *Friend of Edward 7ᵗʰ (1901-1910).*
- ➢ *Inherited the Witley Estate in 1885 (he was 18 years of age)*
- ➢ *1ˢᵗ Marriage: Rachel Ann Gurney in 1891- who drowned in Ireland in 1920.*
- ➢ *Break-up of the Estate and the end of the Dudley Era.*
- ➢ *Sir Herbert Smith (1872-1943) – bought Witley Court in 1920.*
- ➢ *Fire 7ᵗʰ September 1937.*

*Early 19 thCentury watercolour showing the entrance front, chapel and Nash's portico:-
courtesy of Worcestershire Archives and Archaeology Service (ref: BB87/10414)©*

Colour Plates – Description

* *

Introduction:

Witley Court was at one time one of England's most stunning country houses; even today although only a shell of its former grandeur it remains deeply evocative. After the tragic fire of 1937 the then owner Sir Herbert Smith decided not to rebuild but to put the estate up for sale. Witley was never lived in again but tragically was also stripped of anything of value and abandoned to the vandals.

Today despite its ruined state visitors get a rare chance to see the bare bones of a mansion that had grown over the centuries from a substantial Jacobean house, based on the original mediaeval manor house, through the lives of the first *Baron Foley* and his son in the 1720s and 1730s to the addition of the splendid porticos on the north and south sides by *John Nash*, and the ground laid out by possibly *Capability Brown* himself.

The mansion reached the peak of its grandeur and was transformed from a fine mansion to a Victorian Palace in the 1850s with the extensive remodelling commissioned by the first earl of Dudley (2nd creation) from the Architect *Samuel Daukes* with the rich interiors being planned and created by the Royal decorators *Moxon*. This was following the fashion evoked by Queen Victoria at *Osborne House* on the Isle of Wight which was built between 1845 and 1851 to the designs of Prince Albert.

Osborne House on the Isle of Wight - designed by Prince Albert

The vast wealth of the Ward family, later *Earls of Dudley*, who owned the Witley Court estate between 1837 and 1920, derived their wealth from a number of different sources. These included landed estates, industrial enterprises and their plantations in Jamaica. The immense revenue generated allowed Lord Dudley to spend on a lavish scale at Witley Court and to live an extraordinary opulent life, which we in the 21th century can only imagine.

Besides the house itself, the family income allowed the transformation of the gardens at the Court which were designed by *William Andrews Nesfield*, the leading garden designer of his day.

An army of servants and a large number of gardeners looked after the Court itself, while the Dudleys employed many hundreds of people in the various enterprises both on the land and in the industrial 'Black Country'.

Thankfully with the takeover of the Court by *English Heritage* in 1976 much of the grounds and the house have been preserved for the present and for the future. Without their invaluable support Witley Court would like so many other country houses of this period have disappeared into history for ever.

Chapter One – Beginnings

W. Niven in his 1873 '*Old Worcestershire Houses*' gives a description of *Witley Court* which summarises the background to this splendid Victorian palace:

'*Witley Court belonged to the ancient family of Cooksey, from whom it descended in the female line to the Russells of Strensham. It became by purchase the property and seat of the 1ˢᵗ Lord Foley towards the end of the last century. The Elizabethan house was much altered and added to by the last named proprietor, and Earl Dudley, the present owner, has replaced the old part by a mansion in a kind of Italian style from the designs of Mr. Daukes. The house as it appears towards the end of the last century is illustrated in Nash, and in Angus 'Views – 1787'. The plan of the old front is symmetrical with a centre part, with two wings projecting from it. In the angles formed by the wings were placed square towers; the entrance in the centre, and the wings terminated with bay-windows. The house was thus described in 1814: 'an immense white building, consisting of a centre and two projecting wings: the back (sic) has an elegant airy colonnade; but the south front is the principal one, possessing a most superb elevation in a very chaste style of architecture.*'

An early view of Witley Court from the south-east with John Nash's fine portico in pride of place. (Watercolour between 1817-1837) (Ref: BB87/10413): courtesy of the Worcestershire Archives and Archaeology Service©

In 1837 Witley Court and the other Foley estates close by were bought for the incredible sum of £680,000 (2005: £29,988,000.00- National Archives Converter) by the Trustees of the 11ᵗʰ Baron Ward of Birmingham, who was at the time only a minor aged 20. The estates that came with the court included the greater part of *Holt, Shrawley, Witley, Martley* and *Shelsey,* as well as some land in *Kidderminster.*

The Barony of Ward dated back to March 1644. The first holder was a London goldsmith and banker, *Humble Ward* and in 1763 his descendant was created first Viscount Dudley and then Ward. His promotion was largely due to a vast increase in his wealth due to the iron and coal deposits found underneath the property brought into the family by Frances, the wife of the first baron. John William Ward, 1ˢᵗ Earl of Dudley (1781-1833) – died unmarried in an asylum aged 51. His viscounties and his earldom became extinct on his death, while he was succeeded in his junior title of Baron Ward by his 2ⁿᵈ cousin the Rev. William Humble Ward.

There is a collection of letters from The Earl of Dudley to The Bishop of Llandaff published in 1840, with a face page of the Earl- and his quote that '*he neither drinks, hunts, shoots nor fishes*' which is most unusual for a nobleman of the time.

Thanks to the late Nelly Copson of Droitwich©

William Humble Ward. 1ˢᵗ Earl of Dudley (2ⁿᵈ Creation)

William Humble Ward, 11ᵗʰ Lord Ward, 1ˢᵗ Earl (2ⁿᵈ Creation) of *Dudley & Viscount Ednam*, was born on the 27ᵗʰ March, 1817. He was the son of the *Reverend William Humble, Baron Ward of Birmingham* (1781-1835), and Amelia. The Reverend William became the 10th Baron, and although he enjoyed this title, did not have the opportunity to enjoy the wealth which had to be put into trust for his son, who was then a minor. When William Humble Ward died in 1833, his son another William was only 16 and did not come into his full inheritance until aged 28 in 1846.

His trustees purchased, among other properties, *Witley Court* and its estates in Worcestershire in 1837 for around £680,000 (c. £40,800,000 today) with money he had inherited from his trust fund.

It was during this period from 1838 to 1846 the Court was let and from 1843 to 1846 it was leased to *Queen Adelaide* the dowager of *King William IV*. This started a connection with royalty which lasted throughout this period and into the 2nd Earl's time with the visits of Prince Albert and Princess Alexandra the future Edward VIIth and his Queen.

An early drawing of Queen Adelaide

On taking up his inheritance Lord Ward set about remodelling the house to make it into one of the most sumptuous palaces in the country. It was said he spent over £250,000 on the remodelling of the Court equivalent to approximately £15,000,000 today.

Lord Ward's wealth and continuing large revenues came from coal mines, ironworks and other major industries created by the Industrial Revolution.

Besides *Witley Court* and *Himley* Hall, the Dudleys owned *Dudley House* at 100 Park Lane and later *No 7 Carlton Gardens* just off Pall Mall. They owned property and land in *Cheshire, Scotland, Wales*, and *Ireland* and in *France at Boulogne, Nice, Rome,* and *Vienna* and also owned a plantation in *Jamaica*.

The principal plantation was the *Whitney* estate of over three thousand acres, at Clarendon on the edge of the Mocho Mountains. This land came into the Ward family through the marriage to an heiress of the Carver family, descendants of the original settler. The area was known for its fertile soil and the Wards grew coffee, sugar cane, cocoa and bananas. One hundred and fifty eight acres was given over to sugar cane, which was processed to produce both sugar and rum. This estate was worked by 270 slaves until the abolition of the Slave Trade c.1807.

Illustration of the Whitney estate by James Hakewill in his 'Picturesque Tour in the island of Jamaica in 1825'©

By 1883 the English and Welsh Estates totalled over 25,554 acres of which more than 14,000 acres were in Worcestershire. With the additional income from coal mines and other industries the annual income would have exceeded £123,000 or in the region of £7,000,000 today.

William Humble Ward: - courtesy of Dudley Archives©

William Humble Ward attended *Christ Church*, and then *Trinity College* in Oxford in 1835, and although he left without gaining a degree, he was still making a fortune from over 200 mines, mineral resources and the ironworks that he owned.

Where did the Dudley Wealth come from?

The trust's most significant achievement was to purchase extensive landed estates in *Worcestershire, Scotland and Wales.* This was an important long-term move because the value and income of the *Black Country* properties and industrial interests had begun to decline towards the end of the nineteenth century as production costs increased with the exhaustion of the more valuable mineral seams. The trustees' decision to diversify was an important element in ensuring the continued prosperity of the Dudley family interests.

An enigmatic photograph of one of the Earl of Dudley's Collieries, Himley: - courtesy of Ray Jones© - www.surfworcester.co.uk

It must be remembered that although the Dudley estates were extensive compared to other landed aristocracy, Lord Dudley's estates remained relatively small. *Roberts'* survey shows that in 1824 Lord Dudley owned approximately 10,000 acres of which 6,646 acres were agricultural and cottage property. This was situated in and around the *Black Country*. Subsequent purchases of isolated plots of mineral-bearing land increased this to 11,216 acres by 1873. Taking into account the land and property bought by the trust before the 2ⁿᵈ Earl came into his inheritance the property had increased to 25,554 acres at the time of his death in 1885. Even though this appears to be a large landholding, the net income of £123,176 (2005: £7,377,010.64) was exceeded by only six other titled families, all of whom owned over 100,000 acres. These were the *Buccleuch, Devonshire, Northumberland, Bute, Sunderland and Fitzwilliam estates* - (Burke's Peerage, IV, 491).

Lord Ward's wealth had also been due to expansion during the 1820s when *John William, Fourth Viscount Dudley and Ward (created Earl of Dudley in 1827)* purchased estates in *Wales and Scotland*. Probably Lord Dudley at this time wished to broaden the basis of his income beyond the narrow geographical area of the *Black Country* and invest in agricultural property to enhance the family's social and economic status.

Two of the major properties were purchased in Scotland - at *Ednam in Roxburghshire* and *Glengarry in Inverness-shire*. In Wales a large estate was purchased at *Crogen* in the

Dee Valley near *Bala*. By the time of the Earl's death in 1885, his investments in government and overseas stock had produced a considerable income.

The decision to buy the *Witley estate* in 1837 for the Dudley family came after Sir Stephen Glynne formed the *Oak Farm Iron Works Company*, with one of the subsequent shareholders being his brother-in-law, *W. E. Gladstone*, and started to construct furnaces on the site. As *'Himley Hall'* the traditional home of the Dudley family was close by, it became virtually uninhabitable. The noise and fumes caused by the nearby furnaces, coke ovens and engine houses at *Oak Farm*, may have been the impetus for the trustees to look for another estate which could become the family residence. Lord Ward certainly looked on Witley in this light when it came on the market in 1838. Local mineral bearing land was purchased by the trustees at a cost of £25,000 (2005: £1,102,500.00).

Additions were made to the Welsh estate at Crogen in the Dee valley near Bala, purchased by the late earl 'as a matter of fancy' (Hatherton, Col. D260/M/F/5/19/11. Exeter to Hatherton, 5th December 1835). The trustees owned land along a continuous stretch of the river almost from Corwen down to Bala, a distance of about thirteen miles.

The second area where property was purchased in 1836-7 was *Kidderminster*. These were Lord Foley's estates at *Hurcot* for £135,000 and *Oldington* for £89,000.

About this time a survey of the *Witley Court estate* was submitted to the trustees, and did not include land owned in the counties of *Herefordshire*, other parts of *Worcestershire* and *Shropshire*; the agreed purchase price for the whole estate was c. £680,000.

It is interesting that the young Lord Ward enjoyed spending money and one of the Trustees reminded him of his gambling debts at £16,000 (2005: £705,600,000) and urged him not to renew his subscription to *Crockfords*.

Crockfords

Crockfords was a London Gentlemen's club which was initially sited at 50 St James's Street, London and then later at 30 Curzon Street in Mayfair (est.1828).

Founded by *William Crockford*, it was one of the oldest of the London Gentlemen's Clubs. It was centred on gambling and maintained a somewhat raffish and raucous reputation. Between 1874 and 1976 it was home to the *Devonshire Club*.

William Crockford was born in 1775, the son of William and Mary Crockford and was baptised at *St Clement Dane* on the 12th February 1776. He started life working in his father's fish shop adjoining Temple Bar. His fine ability for calculation was soon to stand him in good stead, for he quickly took to gambling and after a number of long sessions amassed a quite considerable fortune. He then launched himself into the London Regency clubland, acquiring a site in St James's Street and opened a building that was to become the most famous gaming house in London- *'Crockfords'*. He fleeced the aristocracy and in the process accumulated a great fortune, certainly enough to establish homes at *11 Carlton*

House Terrace (later to become Prime Minister William Gladstone's home) and at *Panton House*, Newmarket.

He married Sarah Frances Douglas on the 20th May 1812 in *St. Georges Hanover Square;* fathered 14 children and died on 24th May 1844. He is buried in a family vault underneath the *Chapel of Kensal Green Cemetery*, London.

50 St James's Street – Crockfords' first location

The financial arrangements for the purchase of the *Witley estate* by the trustees were that they should pay £331,000 of the total cost of the *Witley estate* by March 1845; until then to pay 4 per cent annual interest on this debt which amounted to £13,477 11s. 2d. There were dangers which became evident as the *Dudley estate* revenue at this time had slumped with the decline in the iron trade in 1841-2, as debts owed to the Dudley estate for minerals purchased mounted, while Lord Ward, himself complicated the situation by borrowing £15,000 (c. £750,000) to pay off his gambling debts and also contracted to purchase the *Invergarry* estate in Scotland for £95,000 (c.£4,750,000). He did this on the basis of an income of £9,000 (£450,000) from that portion of the *Witley estate* which he had contracted to purchase, £2,500 (c.£125,000) from the *Ednam estate* which he enjoyed in his own right as it had been excluded from the trust by the late earl's will, and £2,200 income from the Invergarry estate. In addition he received an annual income of £8,000 (c.£400,000) under the terms of the will.

In 1848 Lord Ward came into his inheritance at last and set about changing his fine new mansion into a Victorian Palace.

An early photograph of Witley Court c.1860-1900.Showing the pristine building soon after completion with the gardens still in infancy: - courtesy of Ray Jones© - www.surfworcester.co.uk

His first marriage was to *Selina Constance De Burgh* (daughter of Hubert De Burgh Esq.) on April 24th 1851. The marriage only lasted for 7 months when his wife died of premature childbirth on November 14th, 1851.

An article appeared in the *Berrow's Worcester Journal* on Thursday, May 1st 1851 concerning the marriage and makes for interesting reading:

NUPTIALS OF LORD WARD AND MISS DE BURGH

'On Thursday last the marriage of this Nobleman with Miss de Burgh, eldest daughter of Robert de Burgh Esq., of West Drayton, was solemnised at St George's Church, Hanover Square, London; the officiating Clergyman being the Rev. Thomas Leigh Claughton, Vicar of Kidderminster, and brother-in-law of Lord Ward. In consequence of a death having unfortunately occurred lately in Mr. de Burgh's family, it was decided that the ceremony should be performed as privately as possible, but for which fact there would have been a large attendance at the Church, as the event had been looked forward to with much interest.

Half- past nine was the time fixed for the celebration to take place, but before that hour, the Noble Lord was in attendance accompanied by his mother, the Lady Ward, the Hon.

Mr. and Mrs. Dudley Ward and some personal friends. The bride arrived with her mother a few minutes before the appointed time, and after receiving the congratulations of her friends, took the arm of her father, and moved to the altar. She wore a superb dress of white 'Gros de Naples', trimmed with the richest point lace, a veil of the same beautiful material extending from the head to the feet, and a wreath of orange blossoms; and was supported by a train of six bridesmaids, attired in white dresses and light blue scarfs. These were the Hon. Frederica and Nina Blake (daughters of Lord Wallascourt). Miss Ward and Miss Claughton (nieces of Lord Ward), and two sisters of the bride.

At the termination of the ceremony, which was very impressively performed, the noble bride and bridegroom retired to the vestry, where the usual record of the marriage was made and attested. The fair bride, who is described as being exquisitely beautiful, was much affected several times during the service. At ten o'clock Lord and Lady Ward returned in Mr. De Burgh's carriage to that gentleman's residence in Grosvenor Crescent, where a select circle partook of breakfast. The happy pair left town early in the day for Sandgate on the Kentish coast, where his Lordship has taken a villa for a few weeks, intending to return to town for the season in early June.

Her Ladyship wore a necklace composed of sapphires of the largest size, with diamond drops and pearls of great value, forming part of a trousseau of jewels presented by her noble husband. When completely fitted out its cost is estimated at about £10,000 (c£440,000). His Lordship's present also included a silver gilt toilette dressing case - a travelling case - a workbox, fitted with pearls and fine gold, and a blotting book, inset in emeralds and rubies, valued at 300 guineas (c£13,200) All these magnificent articles were furnished by Mr. Hancock, of Bruton Street, formerly a partner in the establishment of Messrs Storr and Mortimer.

Rejoicing in the Country

The tenants and friends of the Noble Lord determined to celebrate the auspicious event of his nuptials simultaneously in the several neighbourhoods. We give a sketch of the festivities which occurred in the various localities.

Witley

There was not a person in the parish to whom the day was not one of rejoicing, for by means of a subscription set on foot by the worthy Rector, the Rev. Thomas Pearson and the principal farmers, every one of the poorer neighbours were provided with a good dinner on the occasion, 360lbs of prime beef being distributed in portions varying from 3lbs. to 7lbs. To as many as 75 poor families; 60 gallons of cider were also given away at the same time. This judicious mode of celebration was adopted in preference to a project at first entertained of having old English games and sports on Woodbury Hill. It may be almost needless to state that the health of Lord Ward and his bride were warmly drunk by the peasantry.

Holt

By the invitation of John Pickernell Esq. the tenant of Holt castle and principal occupier of land under Lord Ward, in this part of the country, about 46 persons (farmers from Holt, Little Witley and others; including every one employed on the estate) assembled round the festive board in the hall, and partook in the hospitalities of their kind entertainer. The healths of the noble pair were pledged in ample bumpers and most cordial wishes expressed for their present and future happiness. After dinner the peasantry amused themselves with a variety of rural pastimes on the greensward adjoining the Castle.

At the village of Hillhampton, the tenants of six farms, all of which belong to Lord Ward, provided a sheep which was roasted and subsequently cut up and distributed among their labourers. At the moment of distribution a cannon which had occasionally 'waked echo from her slumbers' during the morning by its discharge being overloaded burst, but fortunately no person was injured by the accident.

Dinner at the Hundred House Inn Witley

In celebration of the wedding the greater part of the tenantry on the Witley Estates dined together in the above Inn, where a most excellent repast was provided by the respected landlord Mr. Arthur.

.... After the proposition of the usual loyal toasts the Chairman rose and said he had to propose a toast which in that house would, he was sure, ever receive a cordial welcome, and on this occasion more especially would they honour it with their loudest cheer and fullest bumper- it was the health of 'Lord and Lady Ward'.....

Himley

This quiet little village, in the immediate vicinity of which is his Lordship's mansion, presented on Thursday last, an unusually animated and bustling appearance, by the crowds of persons who assembled to witness and participate in the rejoicings. From break of day the bells of the parish church sent forth merry peal and occasionally were to be heard loud reports of cannon, which were being discharged from the adjoining park. Connected with the latter demonstration of rejoicing we are extremely sorry to record a melancholy accident, which resulted in the death of a pensioner, named James Sidaway, of Oldswinford, to whom with several other pensioners the care of the field pieces had been confided. About eleven o'clock on the occasion of the 6th round of cannon being discharged, one of the guns exploded, owing it was said to being overcharged, and a piece of the metal (the cannon being shattered into many pieces) struck the ill-fated man on the breast, which penetrating several inches, produced, we are sorry to state almost instant death. At the time of the fatal occurrence the poor man wore a medal of honour on his breast, he having been in the battle of Waterloo, and also in the Peninsular and American *wars. This unhappy circumstance tended to mar the festivities to some extent. The feeling of alarm created by this fatal occurrence was not a little increased by a fire breaking out in the Himley Arms Hotel, the chief seat of the festivities, this verifying the truth of the old adage that 'misfortunes seldom come singly.' Luckily the fire, which was discovered about four o' clock p.m........*

The festivities which had been interrupted by the excitement consequent upon the occurrences were again resumed. Dancing on the greensward, racing, jumping in the bag, and other rustic sports, formed the staple of the entertainments. The children of the Day and Sunday Schools were not forgotten; the former, to the number of 100, being treated with an abundant and excellent dinner in the schoolroom, (where they were visited by some of the ladies and gentry of the neighbourhood) and the latter, together with such as chose to partake of the hospitality this provided by his Lordship's tenantry out of respect for him, and in honour of the festive occasion, to the number of upwards of 400, were bountifully regaled with a substantial dinner on the green, with a liberal allowance of ale, many of the tenantry officiating as carvers and waiters. The approach to the Himley Arms either way was decorated in an elegant manner, with triumphant arches of evergreens and artificial flowers, and at dusk they were illuminated with coloured lamps, in different devices, with the words 'May happiness attend them.'.....During the evening splendid displays of fireworks were exhibited in the park...Himley Hall was brilliantly illuminated. A sumptuous dinner was provided at 7 o'clock at the Himley Arms, to which about 60 influential gentry of the village and neighbourhood sat down. The customary toasts were proposed and duly honoured; the toast of the evening experiencing a most enthusiastic reception. The festivity of the party was kept up to a late hour.' Sedgley and other parts of the Dudley Estate held similar celebrations for the wedding.

An interesting insight into the personality of the First Earl came from a book entitled 'My Recollections' by Countess Cardigan and Lancastre - published in 1909: *'....William Ward was a pleasant man, but he had extraordinary ideas of how to treat a wife......poor Constance was not very tactful and not accommodating. Her husband worshipped the beautiful; he had selected his wife partly on account of her beauty, and treated her like some lovely slave he had bought. He had a strange, almost barbaric passion for precious stones, and he bought quantities of them and lavished them on his wife, who appeared at great entertainments literally ablaze with diamonds.*

What pleased Lord Ward more than anything was to make Constance put on all her jewels for his special benefit when they were alone. He would admire her thus for hours, delighting in her lovely unclothed figure, and contrasting the sheen of her ropes of pearls with her delicate skin, as she sat on a black satin covered couch.'

Throughout the 1850s William contributed enthusiastically to the building of churches, and education establishments, and to the expansion of industry, by founding the *Round Oak Steel Works Ltd.*

The Round Oak Steel Works c. 1868

He was created *Earl of Dudley* and *Viscount Ednam* on February 13th 1860. His second marriage was to an 18 year old socialite *Georgina Elizabeth Moncrieffe* (third daughter of Sir Thomas Moncrieffe) on November 21st, 1865. The Earl was 48 years of age, so there was an age gap of 30 years.

'A carte-de-visite portrait of society beauty Georgina Moncrieffe dressed as Mary, Queen of Scots. The historical tableau here depicted shows the Scottish queen with her ladies-in-waiting, known as 'The Four Mary's' (Mary Seaton, Mary Beaton, Mary Fleming and Mary Livingstone). This photograph was taken at the Braemar Gathering in 1863 - two years before Georgina became the new Countess of Dudley. The Prince and Princess of Wales first attended the Braemar Gathering in 1863. The event is held on the first Saturday in September to this day. Large crowds gather to celebrate their Monarch as Chieftain of the gathering where pipe music, dance and games make for a wonderful atmosphere. On that occasion, the royal couple stayed at Mar Lodge, the Highland residence of the Earl and Countess of Fife.

The photograph was taken at the Braemar Gathering in the grounds of Mar Lodge in August 1863 during the first official visit to Scotland by the Prince and Princess of Wales. At the celebrations which followed the games, the Prince and Princess were entertained by a series of tableaux vivants and scenes from amateur theatricals staged by the other guests.' (Photograph and description by courtesy of Ray Jones –www.surfworcester.co.uk)

The 1st Earl of Dudley (1817-1885) and his second wife Georgina Elizabeth Moncrieffe: - courtesy of Dudley Archives©

1874.   ADÈLE.

Georgina Elizabeth Moncrieffe – Countess of Dudley- photographed by Adele in 1874:-courtesy of Ray Jones© www.surfworcester.co.uk

The Worcester Journal of Saturday November 25th 1865 featured an article on the marriage of the Earl of Dudley:

'The marriage of the Earl of Dudley to Georgina Elizabeth, third daughter of Sir Thomas and Lady Louisa Moncrieffe, was celebrated on Tuesday at St. Paul's, Knightsbridge.

It was estimated that there were nearly 2000 persons in and around St. Paul's Church on the morning the ceremony was performed, and the services of a body of police, under the command of Inspector Rolles, were called into requisition to keep the path clear for the entrance of the bridal party, and the ladies and gentlemen who were admitted to witness the ceremony.

.... The guests included Lady Ward, the Countess of Kinnou, Mr. and Mrs. Lady Charlotte Russell, the Marchioness of Ely, the Marquis of Queensberry, the Earl and Countess of Westmorland, the French Ambassador, his Excellency the Prince de la Tour d' Auvergne, accompanied by the Marquis de Tamisier, Prince Edward of Saxe Weimar, the Duchess of Buccleuch, Mr. Alfred Rothschild, &c.

St. Paul's Church, Knightsbridge, London

The bridal party proceeded to the residence of the Countess of Kinnoul, the bride's grandmother, in Belgrave Square, where a sumptuous dejeuner was spread for the bridal party, with a few other friends not present at the ceremony. The bill of fare was as follows:

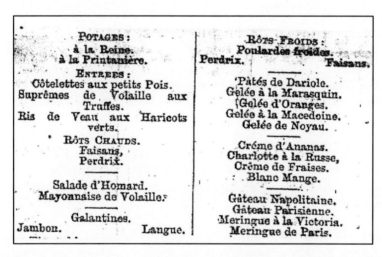

The tables were elegantly laid out and decorated with flowers &c. The bride cake was not large, but the design was elegant. Before the company retired from the dining room, Lord Rokeby rose and proposed in a few sentences 'The Health and Happiness of the bride and bridegroom.'

PRESENTS TO THE BRIDE:

The array of presents to the bride, set out in the drawing room at the residence of the Bride's father was a magnificent one. The presents were of almost all kinds, but the more important ones that need to be noticed here:

Lord Dudley: A matchless parure consisting of a diadem, necklace, brooch, earrings and bracelets, consisting of rubies and diamonds of the finest quality-the rubies specimen stones- set in pure classical style and most elegant in form being at the same time entirely a work of art in diamond setting. The value was nearly £10,000 (c.£450,000). There was also a pair of very fine sapphire and diamond earrings; a locket and brooch to match, with fine pearl drop; a pearl and diamond bracelet; a pair of pearl and diamond pear-shaped earrings; a jewelled Etruscan suite. A diamond necklace, with pearl and diamond drops. Five brilliant diamond stars, head ornaments. Diamond locket. Three bracelets set with pearls and diamonds. A bracelet with a large diamond of fabulous value in the centre. Sprays of roses in diamonds, and other brilliants for the hair. A work-box inlaid with gold and pearls, a dressing case and other ornaments for the boudoir.

Lady Ward: A very handsome miniature bracelet, with monogram on cover in rubies, emeralds and diamonds; with a superb silver-gilt dressing case studded with stones. Lady Kinnoul's gift was a writing desk; the Hon. Mrs. Anson presented Sevres vases; Miss Moncrieffe, china vases; the Hon. Mrs. Claughton; pearl and diamond bracelet; the Baroness Rothchild, a gold bracelet; Lady Fitzgerald, a book stand; Mr. W. C. Heming, a Sevres china clock.'

Celebrations to mark the wedding took place at Dudley, Kidderminster, Bewdley, Brierley Hill, Hillhampton, Holt, Perth, Llandrillo and Llandderfel and other places associated with the Dudley interests. In Witley:

'Mr. Richard Smith, nurseryman of this city, presented a magnificent specimen of the Wellington gigantean to the Earl and Countess, which was planted by Mr. Claughton jun., in the park at Witley on Tuesday. There were no public festivities here, as they will come off on his Lordship's return home.'

The Berrow's gives a detailed description of both the wedding itself and the homecoming to *Witley Court* - celebrations took part in the towns associated with the Dudleys. Here is an interesting description from Worcester when the children from *All Saints* celebrated the wedding and homecoming:

'The school treat to the children of All Saints was proposed by Mr. Haywood, seedsman and churchwarden of the parish, who made a collection among the parishioners for the purpose, and in the afternoon the infants numbering 100, were regaled with plum cake and an orange each and sent home, while all above five years of age were invited to assemble in the school room at five o'clock, which had been very tastefully decorated by the rector and teachers with banners, flags, mottoes &c. A plentiful supply of plum cake and tea was provided, and afterwards the rector, the Rev. R. Arthure, gave a reading from a moral fable which much amused the little ones. A song followed by Mr. J.H. White, which was greatly applauded. Other readings and songs followed, but the great event of the evening was when Mr. Haywood filled the little ones with amazement by exhibiting Pharaoh's Serpents. Afterwards the rector amused all very much by various scenes comic and instructive from a magic lantern.....'

All Saints Church in Worcester:-JRH

In December of the same year the City of Worcester presented the couple with a cabinet service to celebrate their marriage. *The Royal Porcelain Works* also made a duplicate set for display to the public:

Countess of Dudley Royal Porcelain Service: - courtesy of Royal Worcester Porcelain Archives©

In the Phillips Auction Catalogue for 6th December 1995 appeared the following entry:

'Thomas Scott Callowhill and Samuel Ranford: An important Royal Worcester Teapot made as a duplicate for the Countess of Dudley Service, the French shape raised on three gilt lion paw feet, decorated with a myriad of tiny turquoise jewels in graduated sizes on a solid gold ground with further gold dots between, the reserved panels on each side painted with a classical female head in profile also on a gold ground and framed with tiny white jewels, 13.5cm. high, unmarked c.1875-77 (handle broken into three sections and restuck, a few jewels missing on the handle and a small area of jewels damaged on the body-£1500-£1800).

It is not certain how many duplicates were made during the 1870s but at least three teapots are recorded, all slightly different in design. The original set made as a wedding gift for the Earl and Countess of Dudley was one of the first productions of the Worcester factory. Made in 1865, it was lent by the Earl for the Parish Exhibition in 1867 and subsequently the factory borrowed it again to make duplicates.' – 'Thanks to Royal Worcester Porcelain Archives for permission to use these illustrations©'

The teapot from the Countess of Dudley Service: - courtesy of Royal Worcester Porcelain Archives© - (See colour plate)

A description of the new Lady Dudley at the time of her marriage was given by Mrs. Berkeley, the mistress of Cotheridge Court, who as a girl had presented a bouquet to Lady Dudley on her homecoming as a new bride:

'It is no question of preferring blonde to dark, tall to petite, pallid or vivid in colouring, Georgina was just apart from everybody. Her mass of rich auburn hair, her height, her stateliness, her matchless complexion and above all her charm made an indelible impression on all who saw her.'

Georgina Countess of Dudley:-courtesy of Ray Jones© www.surfworcester.co.uk

Life at Witley Court was at this time at its most magnificent and extravagant as Mrs Berkeley remembers:

'The Christmas trees and parties of those days at Witley Court were truly a vision of magnificence. For three consecutive years strings of jewels hung from branches of the tree, and twice I had the first choice.'

The magnificent Christmas tree in the Ballroom at Witley Court c.1913:- courtesy of Ray Jones©
www.surfworcester.co.uk (see colour plate)

RUSSELL & SONS
29 UNION ROAD,   LONDON, N.W &
TUFNELL PARK.   EAST ST. CHICHESTER.
PHOTOGRAPHERS TO THE ROYAL FAMILY.

The Countess of Dudley with four of her children:-courtesy of Ray Jones© -

The Earl of Dudley died of pneumonia on the 7th May, 1885; he was 68 years of age. He was buried in a fine tomb at *Great Witley Church*, but his body was later exhumed and reburied in *Worcester Cathedral* in 1953. He left an estate worth £1,026,000 (c. £61,560,000 today). A statue was erected in his memory at the junction of *Castle Hill* and

Castle Street in *Dudley*. He was succeeded by his son, *William Humble Ward the 2ᵈ Earl*.

The Statue of the 1st Earl of Dudley (2nd Creation) in Dudley

Some of the notable incidents which stand out most markedly in his career are the following:

1. *The Rescue of Kidderminster.* In 1855 the trade of that town seemed doomed, owing to the introduction of steam power for making carpets. The hand weavers were being reduced into great poverty. Lord Ward, as he was then, came to their rescue; found the necessary capital to enable the manufacturers to build new sheds and place in them the most up to date machinery driven by steam power, and thus enabled the people to save the carpet industry for Kidderminster.

2. *Voyage to the Crimea.* Along with the rest of England, Lord Ward's indignation was aroused by the appalling descriptions which the celebrated war correspondent *Sir W. Russell* gave of the troops in the Crimea; suffering due to mismanagement. Lord Ward fitted up a large vessel, filled it with comforts for the soldiers, and went himself to see that the help was properly administered.

3. A keen philanthropist, Lord Ward established a *reformatory school for the children of criminals,* so that they might not follow in their fathers' footsteps. It was Lord Ward who also advocated the conversion of the *Arboretum* area of *Worcester City* into a grand public park, offering to contribute to the cost. Unfortunately, the short-sighted members of the Corporation, who could see no further than a possible increase in rates, combined with those who had private

interests to serve, and defeated the project. Houses were built on the proposed site instead.

4. Lord Dudley was also the founder of the Worcester School of Art

William Earl of Dudley and Viscount Ednam (1817-1885):- courtesy of Dudley Archives©

It was in 1860 that the public services of Lord Ward were recognised by the revival of the old family titles, and his lordship was created *Earl of Dudley and Viscount Ednam*.

The earl was a keen churchman, contributing to the support of many churches; but the greatest exercise of his munificence was in connection with the restoration of *Worcester Cathedral* which took place between 1855-1875.

Worcester Cathedral Tower:- JRH©

Worcester Cathedral in December 2010:- JRH©

The Cathedral Restoration contribution by Lord Dudley

In 1855- when *Peel* was Dean, and *Benson, Somers-Cox, Fortescue and Woods* were Canons- a new era began, and *Mr. Perkins*, the architect was commissioned to execute extensive repairs at the east end. In 1857 a fine of £5,000 (c. £300,000) was received in connection with a lease, and instead of dividing it among themselves, the Chapter decided to devote the whole to the repair and restoration of the Cathedral. The inartistic east window was removed and replaced by one designed by Mr. Perkins. The whitewash was scraped off the Lady Chapel and Choir and the marble columns shown in their true colours.

In 1859 the notable Victorian architect *Sir George Gilbert Scott* was called in, and approved of Mr. Perkins's proposals for further restoration. In this year the Cathedral estates were transferred to the *Ecclesiastical Commissioners*, part of the bargain being that the sum of £15,000 (c.£90,000) be paid over for the restoration of the Cathedral.

The work of restoration went on steadily until 1864, the sum of £31,000 (c. £1,860,000) having been expended out of the capitular funds; but much remained to be done. As the Chapter had exhausted their available resources, it was decided to request *Lord Lyttelton*, as *Lord Lieutenant*, to appeal to the public for subscriptions in order that the rearrangement of the choir might be carried out according to the report presented, to the Dean and Chapter by Sir Gilbert Scott in November, 1863.

On April 7ᵗʰ 1864 a meeting was held in the *Guildhall*, under the presidency of Lord Lyttelton; the Bishop, *Lord Dudley*, Sir John Pakington from Westwood House, Sir Edmund Lechmere, the Dean and Canons and a large number of persons were present. The subscription contributed at this meeting amounted to £12,000 (c. £720,000); half of this was contributed by *Lord Dudley*, on condition that the tower be included in the scheme, which would add another £8,000 (c. £480,000) to the cost. *Lord Dudley* expressed the hope that if the Cathedral were restored as a house of prayer, the *Three Choirs Festival* would no longer be held in the Cathedral nave. The Dean and Chapter, although they sympathised with the Earl, could not guarantee this, but nevertheless *Lord Dudley* continued with his benevolence, although he did state that when the tower was restored no clock was to be placed on the outside of the tower. Thankfully his wishes were honoured.

The work of the Great Restoration took twenty-nine years. *'Great was the rejoicing in Worcester when the work was finished; and gay were the decorations throughout the city when on Wednesday April 8ᵗʰ 1874, the opening services were held.'*

The contributions to the restored Cathedral which *Lord Dudley* paid for was firstly the beautiful black and white marble floor of the Nave, which had been substituted for the rough, uneven stone floor. The improvement had cost *Lord Dudley* in the region of £5,000 (c. £300,000). He paid for substituting marble for the white Hopton stone and blue slate similar to that in the cloisters. It was changed from that specified in the original contract.

The magnificent marble Nave pulpit designed by *Sir Gilbert Scott* and sculpted by *Forsyth of Worcester* was another fine contribution to the restored work. *Earl Dudley's* contributions to the Cathedral earned him the right to be buried within its walls. Although interred in a fine tomb in Witley Church, the body was later removed in 1953 to the magnificent marble tomb designed by *Sir Gilbert Scott* and worked by *Forsyth*. It lies proudly in the Lady Chapel opposite an equally fine tomb for Lord Lyttelton. Dean Peel's magnificent altar reredos dedicated to his wife acts as a splendid backdrop.

The magnificent tomb designed by Gilbert Scott and carved by Forsyth of Worcester to Lord Dudley:- courtesy of the Dean and Chapter of Worcester Cathedral©

The finely crafted image of the 1ˢᵗ Lord Dudley by Forsyth of Worcester:- courtesy of the Dean and Chapter of Worcester Cathedral©

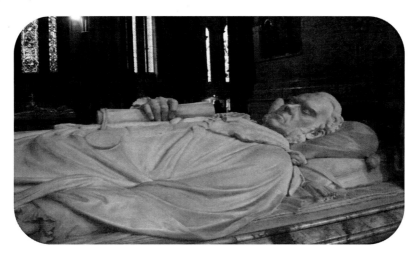

Lord Lyttelton, brother– in-law of Gladstone and ancestor of the present Viscount Cobham, the 4ᵗʰ Lord Lyttelton as Lord Lieutenant of Worcestershire:- courtesy of the Dean and Chapter of Worcester Cathedral©

The first Earl was a director of the *Worcester Porcelain Factory* and entertained many famous figures at Witley Court. Probably the most notable was Prince Albert and Princess Alexandra the future King Edward VIIth and his consort. Here is a picture of the elderly Earl entertaining the Prince at Witley Court- by the look of the muddy boots this was more than likely a shooting party weekend which the Earl and the Prince enjoyed very much.

H.M. Queen Alexandra

Shooting Party at Witley Court with the 1st Earl and Prince Albert:- courtesy of Royal Worcester Porcelain©

Lord Dudley was a shareholder and a director of the Royal Porcelain Works and the Museum has some interesting articles from the Dudley period.

Part of the Chamberlain dinner Service with a large coat of arms from the time of Lord Ward probably from the c.1830s: courtesy of the Royal Worcester Archives©

This is part of the Royal Worcester Collection- a plaster cast head of the 1ˢᵗ Earl, but the archives have no answers as to why it was originally made! : courtesy of Royal Worcester Archives©

Lord Dudley's Obituary appeared in the Times in 1885:

'Lord Dudley died at Dudley-house, Park Lane, early yesterday morning, after an illness of two days, from an attack of pneumonia. Sir William Gull and Mr. F. Manly Sims attended him during his illness.

......*He was born on the 27th of March 1817, and was educated at Eton, whence he removed in due course to Christ Church, Oxford.*

He migrated, however, to Trinity College, being a private pupil of the Rev. Thomas Legh Claughton, then one of the Fellows, afterwards Professor of Poetry at Oxford, and Bishop of Rochester, and now Bishop of St. Albans, who eventually married his lordship's sister. Lord Dudley never had a seat in the House of Commons, having succeeded at the age of 18 to his father's barony of Ward. He never took an active or prominent part in politics; but he was a magistrate and deputy-lieutenant for Worcestershire, and also a magistrate for the county of Stafford.

Dudley House in 2012: JRH©

He sat as chairman of the Worcestershire Quarter Sessions from 1859 till 1880. He was also a Trustee of the National Gallery, and High Steward of Kidderminster. In 1854 he was appointed Lieutenant-Colonel Commandant of the Worcestershire Yeomanry Cavalry, of which regiment he became Honorary Colonel in 1871. Lord Dudley was attached to Earl Granville's special Embassy to Russia in July 1856; and also to the late Earl of Clarendon's special Embassy to Berlin and Konigsberg in October 1861, when he proceeded thither as Her Majesty's Ambassador Extraordinary to the King of Prussia on the occasion of His Majesty's Coronation. In 1860 Lord Ward was advanced by the Premier, Lord Palmerston to the Earldom of Dudley, on account to his having succeeded to a large portion of the wealth and estates of his father's relative, the Last Lord Dudley of the previous creation. Lord Dudley was twice married. His first wife, whom he married in April 1851, was Selina Constance, eldest daughter to the late Mr. Hubert De Burgh, of West Drayton Manor, Middlesex. He was however, left a widower in November of the same year. In 1865 he married Georgina Elizabeth, third daughter of the late Sir Thomas and Lady Moncreiffe, of Moncreiffe, and sister of Sir Robert D. Moncreiffe, the present baronet, and of the Duchess of Atholl. By her he had a family of one daughter and six sons. The title devolves upon his eldest son, William Humble, Viscount Ednam, who was born in 1867. The funeral will take place at Witley Court on Tuesday next. It is stated that Viscount Ednam left England three weeks ago for Rio Janeiro, and is consequently unacquainted with the news of his father's death.

The Mechanics' Institute - Dudley

The news of Lord Dudley's death created a profound impression in Dudley and the districts round about, which have benefited so largely by his enterprise and munificence. The bell of the parish church was tolled during the afternoon, and flags half-mast high were raised in the market-place and at his lordship's Round Oak Iron Works. The late earl conferred many gifts upon Dudley, including a fine fountain in the market-place which cost £3000 and the local Mechanics' Institute, the Guest Hospital, the school and dispensary were largely indebted to his liberality. In Dudley, Worcester, Kidderminster and other places he was a princely benefactor to the Church of England.

The Guest Hospital in Dudley

The Guest Hospital as built on Tipton Road in Dudley and the buildings were originally constructed in 1849 by the Earl of Dudley to accommodate miners blinded in the numerous coal mines in the area belonging to the Earl. The miners rejected the Earl's charity and the buildings remained empty for some 22 years until 1871 when they were taken over by a local chain maker, Joseph Guest and turned into a hospital.

In July 1885 the Times published the will of Lord Dudley which makes for some interesting reading:

'....the value of the personal estate in the United Kingdom amounting to upwards of £1,026,000 (c. £605,34,000). The testator gives to his wife an immediate legacy of £5,000 (c£300,000) all her paraphernalia and the presents made to her on her marriage; and the appropriate guardian of his infant children during their respective minorities. His jewellery and personal ornaments he leaves for the use of his wife for life; then certain of his jewellery of which he gives a list, is to be enjoyed as heirlooms, with the hereditaments limited by the will of John William, Earl of Dudley; and the remainder of his jewellery is to go to his daughter, Lady Edith Ward. He also leaves to his wife an annuity of £2000 (c. £120,000) during the joint lives of herself and his mother, Lady Ward, and on the death of the latter the said annuity is to be increased to £7000 (c. £420,000)per annum; an annuity of £7000 (c£420,000) to his mother, Lady Ward and an annuity of £1500 (c £90,000) to his sister, the Hon. Mrs. Julia Susannah Claughton. These annuities are to be paid, in addition to any other sums the annuitants may be entitled to, out of the estates of which he is tenant for life. He bequeaths £5000 (c. £300,000) to his nephews and nieces...£5000 each to his solicitor, Mr. Benbow and his mining agent Mr. Smith; and legacies to his executors, land agents, domestic servants, gardeners, gamekeepers and stable servants; certain pensions which he has been in the habit of paying, are also to be kept up. £50,000 (c£3,000,000) is to be left in trust for his daughter, and £90,000 (c. £5,400,000)for each of his five sons, in addition to the £60000 (c £3,600,000) they are entitled to receive under the will of John William, Earl of Dudley. The residue of his real and personal estate he leaves to his son or grandson, who shall succeed to the hereditaments under the limitations in the will of the said John William, Earl of Dudley.....

* *

Chapter Two: Witley Court -The Dudley Era 1837-1920

After the departure of *Queen Adelaide* from *Witley Court* in 1846, *Lord Ward,* at the age of 28 and just coming into his inheritance in 1848, came to live at Witley Court. His first task was to plan the remodelling of the house and the grounds and the restoration of the church.

For the house he engaged the architect *Samuel Daukes* and brought down two brothers who were sculptors and woodcarvers from his Scottish estates, *James and William Forsyth.*

Moxon the Royal decorators were brought in to the refurbish the principal rooms in the Second Empire style.

For the landscaping of the gardens and parkland he employed *William Nesfield* whose '*Monster Work'* included two beautifully carved fountains. By the time of his death in 1885, Lord Ward had created a Palladian Palace of such magnificence it became one of the finest Victorian palaces in England.

Samuel Whitfield Daukes' most important country house commission was the remodelling of 'Witley Court' on a gigantic scale in a sumptuous classical style. Two of the designs put forward for the changes were exhibited at the Royal Academy in 1855. Before his work at Witley Court he had worked close by in Great Witley at *Abberley Hall* c.1846 and at *Horstead Place* in Sussex in 1850-1852.

Abberley Hall:-courtesy of Jo Roche©

In the '*Builder'* for February 19th 1859 it was reported that '*very considerable works are being executed at Witley Court for Lord Ward. The house is being improved and fitted up under the direction of Mr. Daukes, architect, and the grounds are being adorned by Mr. W. A. Nesfield. Forming part of the latter works is a basin 180 feet by 120 feet, having in the centre a fountain of large size and cost.....The group represented Perseus and Andromeda, surmounts an octagon basement, 24 feet in diameter, on which are shells and dolphins throwing water, with vases at intervals. It was designed by Mr. Nesfield, and being executed in Portland stone by Mr. Forsyth; Messrs. J. Geefs and A. Waagen having assisted in the modelling. The fountain will be 26 feet high from the water-line and will probably be completed in October next. Messrs. Easton and Co. are the engineers. Mr. Wood of Worcester was the builder employed on the house. The Carton Pierre ornamentation for the ceilings and panelling of the rooms, which by the way, is elaborate, after the style of Louis XVI, was by a Frenchman. Mr. Moxon is the painter and decorator.....'*

At the commencement of the works the *Berrow's Worcester Journal* for Saturday 30th December 1854 reported the events which were taking place just outside the city at Witley:

'External and internal alterations are being made to this mansion on a grand scale, on plans furnished by S. W. Daukes, Esq. of London, formerly of this city. The whole of the exterior of the building, which is at present only plainly cemented, will be cased in Bath stone, and the elevation will be changed for one of Italian character. On Saturday last the workmen engaged in the reparations, and who are in the employment of Mr. Joseph Wood of this city, to whom the execution of these works has been entrusted, were, by the liberality of Lord Ward, regaled with an excellent repast, replete with an abundance of good English cheer. The dinner was provided by Mr. Hambler, in a large marquee erected in the grounds. The usual toasts were duly honoured and the noble entertainer's health was drunk with hearty cheers. The party separated about 6 o'clock highly pleased with their entertainment.'

A very early 'Earl of Worcester' photograph of Witley Court c.1860-1900:- courtesy of Ray Jones©

An early photograph of the Orangery and the Church c.1860-1900:- courtesy of Ray Jones©

Samuel Whitfield Daukes (sometimes Dawkes): 1811-1880

The architect Earl Dudley employed to work on Witley Court was a man who spent his life on a great many enterprises and he is certainly worth looking at in some detail.

Samuel Daukes was born in London in 1811, the son of Samuel Whitfield Daukes, a businessman with interests in coal mining and the brewery trade. He bought *Diglis House* (now the Diglis Hotel) in Worcester in 1827. He was first articled in about 1827 to James Pigott Pritchett of York, and had set himself up in practice in Gloucester by 1834.

The Diglis Hotel in Worcester- 2012:-JRH©

From 1839-42 Daukes was the architect employed by the *Birmingham and Gloucester Railway*, designing clerks' houses, engine sheds, brakemen's cottages and in 1840, *Lansdown station* in Cheltenham. He was also the architect for the *London,Oxford and Cheltenham Railway Company*. Between 1842 and 1848 he started a London office at *14 Whitehall Place*, and he began to build up a large practice in the English Midlands.

Daukes died at Beckenham in Kent in 1880, and was buried in the family vault in *Highgate Cemetery*. Attached to his will was a list of all his architectural books in his office, an eclectic selection, including *Weale's Quarterly Papers in Architecture* as well as all *Pugin's* publications, and the transactions of the *Cambridge Camden Society*; but the charities to which he left money were all low church.

Samuel Daukes' early work appears to be influenced by his family's connections and a link with his future patron Lord Ward was provided by his uncle, *Richard Davies,* who was Lord Ward's mining agent. His family was of good financial standing which enabled him to buy the *Park Estate* in Cheltenham. He was a great admirer of *Pugin* and a long-term member of the *Ecclesiological Society*. He designed churches in the neo-Norman and perpendicular styles. He was able to use these styles at *Abberley Hall, Witley Court and Colney Hatch*, with considerable originality and dash, and he comes across as an architect full of confidence, with a secure command of the picturesque elements of a composition. Daukes failed, however, to adapt to the changing stylistic climate of the *High Victorian* period, and in the 1860s his practice seems to have declined, although he was still building churches in the Midlands.

The list of his major works is extensive but worthy of note are the following:

- *The Park Estate*, Cheltenham in Gloucestershire: he laid out the estate and the zoological gardens for Thomas Billings, 1833-34; Daukes bought this estate himself in 1839.
- *Abberley Hall*, Worcestershire: for J. L. Moilliet, in 1837, in an Italianate style. This building was destroyed by fire in 1845 and reconstructed to a modified design in 1846-49 for Mrs. Moilliet and then altered again c. 1883.

Abberley Hall:

Abberley Hall lies on the actual boundary between Great Witley and Abberley.
The Walsh family held Abberley for 175 years (1532-1707) and one, William, who rose in distinction in the literary field, was a contemporary and friend of Joseph Addison as well as Pope and Dryden.
The manor passed to the Bromleys in 1837. The estate which had been very run-down was sold to John Lewis Moilliet of Birmingham and Geneva.
He employed Samuel Whitfield Daukes to rebuild the house which was at the time called Abberley Lodge. Shortly after its completion in 1845, Moilliet died and soon after his death fire ravaged the Hall, leaving only one tower intact. Dowager Queen Adelaide, who was at the time living at Witley Court, offered accommodation there to Mrs. Moilliet, his widow, but she declined and moved

into the Hundred House and then later to Laugherne House at Martley. Samuel Whitfield Daukes was again employed on the reconstruction.

On Amelia Moilliet's death in 1857, she was succeeded by her son James, who was at the time living at the 'Elms' nearby and who became High Sheriff of Worcestershire in 1861.

Abberley Hall was eventually sold in 1867 along with about eleven hundred acres to Joseph Jones who was a cotton industrialist from Lancashire. He was succeeded by his cousin, John, Joseph Jones in 1880. He added the west wing and a block of stables as well as a theatre and stage. The coach house later became the chapel. As an example of his energy and progressive ideas he mined coal on the estate, had his own gasworks and built a system of waterworks with reservoirs on the Abberley Hill.

In 1883 he erected on Merritts Hill, the gothic clock tower, which contained a carillon which with its six different barrels, played tunes appropriate to the day, every three hours, from a selection of forty-two in addition to chiming the hours and the quarters. Abberley Hall today is a prestigious preparatory school.

- *Lansdown Railway Station in Cheltenham* for the Birmingham and Gloucester Railway Company in 1840. This was in an Italianate style, but the fine portico was removed in the 1960s.

- *Tibberton Court*, in Gloucestershire in 1842 for W. P. Price. Alterations were also planned but perhaps never executed.

- *Royal Agricultural College at Cirencester*: 1845-48.

Royal Agricultural College at Cirencester (c)

Tibberton Court in Gloucestershire

- *Bricklehampton Hall* in Worcestershire in an Italianate style for Francis Woodward.
- *The Abbey Hotel*, in Great Malvern in a Jacobean style from 1848-49. He also designed the *Holy Trinity Church* at Link Top in Malvern in 1850-51.
- *Dudley House*, in Park Lane, London in 1855 when he designed a new picture gallery for Lord Ward; this was damaged in World War Two but was restored by *Sir Basil Spence* in 1969-70.

The picture gallery at Dudley House, London: courtesy of English Heritage©

- *Great Witley Church* in c.1855 for Lord Ward and extensive alterations to Witley Court in the Italianate style.

Witley Court Church: JRH©

The builders who were employed to carry out the major changes and alterations at Witley Court were *Joseph Wood & Sons of Worcester.*

During the lifetime of the first and second Earls, the park was developed as well as the gardens and a complete change was made to the house. More than 400 deer roamed the park; a cricket ground was laid out inside the park; and an archery green was planned, where numerous county matches were played. In the 1890s a nine hole golf course was laid out.One of the most memorable matches to be played here took place on the 7th February 1902, when the professionals, representing the major English and Scottish clubs, played over 36 holes at Witley.

Joseph Wood & Sons- Builders and Contractors, English and Foreign Timber and Slate Merchants

This Worcester Company carried out some of the largest and most important public and private works in this and in other parts of the Midlands.

The headquarters of the company occupied 2 ½ acres on The Butts, alongside the old cattle market and today alongside the '*Hive'* the new University Library.

The previous premises of J.P. Woods and Sons on the Butts in 2009:- JRH©

The iconic 'Hive' built on the site of the workshops of J. P. Woods and Sons-2012:- JRH©

There were two large gateway entrances from the street, giving admission to the spacious yards, in which were erected the buildings occupied by the various industrial departments.

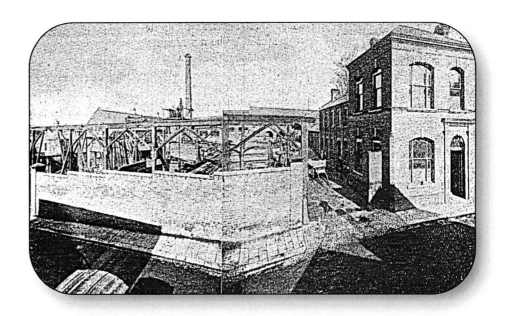

Joseph Woods and Sons (Worcester) Ltd in 1905:- Worcestershire Archives and Archaeology Service©

The principal of the two main buildings contained the sawing, planning and moulding mills.

The power for the works was provided by a powerful steam engine and boiler erected in a separate building; the remaining premises consisted of offices, stores for materials and the massive drying sheds. The yard was spanned by a powerful travelling crane, and the yard was stocked with both home-grown and imported timber held to mature until needed for the various building projects the firm was involved with.

Among the contracts which had been filled by this company were such buildings as the *Victoria Institute* in Worcester, which was a splendid museum, art gallery, library and College of Art for the City. Other fine buildings included the *Worcester and City Bank*, today Lloyds Bank in the centre of the City; the restoration of *St David's Cathedral,* Pembrokeshire; casemented barracks at Milford Haven; the barracks at Wrexham and other buildings for the War Office and Government, together with many of the principal mansions and private residences in both Worcestershire and further afield.

The former Worcester and City Bank at the Cross - today Lloyds Bank:-JRH©

Impney Hall - residence of Mr John Corbett, Esq: - JRH©

These included *Witley Court* the residence of the Right Hon. Earl Dudley; '*Impney Hall*' at Droitwich, the residence of John Corbett, Esq., the mansions for

C.W. Lea, Esq., at Worcester and C.W.D. Perrins, Esq., at Malvern, and the mansion of the Hon. A. P. Allsopp, at *Battenhall Mount* in Worcester.

The company in its heyday employed large numbers of skilled workmen and these could range up to five hundred men depending on the contracts being undertaken at the time.

Battenhall Mount-Worcester: - courtesy of Ray Jones©

The late Nelly Copson of Droitwich, a renowned local historian gave me some sheets written about 100 years ago which gives an insight into the grounds and setting of Witley Court. The descriptions are evocative:

'Having some time on my hands I sauntered through the grounds, the beauty and excellent arrangement of which were a source of admiration, although a December fog, like a thick veil over nature's face, hid half her beauties from me. These grounds were laid out and improved by the late Lord Foley, who had excellent taste and a nice appreciation of landscape gardening: there are sheets of water, and islands, and cascades tumbling and foaming, and undulating surfaces embossed in evergreens, and labyrinthine paths winding their crooked courses among verdant shrubberies, and lofty clustering trees to overlook the whole.

The present approaches were also formed by the late lord, the old entrance leaving the turnpike road in front of the house, passing down an avenue, and crossing the lake over a bridge.

The park consists of about 400 acres, and is well stocked with deer. There are here some gigantic oaks in full vigour- one (which is in decay) near to the south front measures thirty feet in circumference; and I may here add, that immediately on the confines of the parish formerly stood an oak under which St. Augustine is said to have met the monks of Bangor; it was always called St. Augustine's oak, and may possibly have been the spot for such a meeting.'

Witley Court from the grounds c.1882:- courtesy of Worcestershire Archives and Archaeology Service©

Life at Witley Court

The world of above and below stairs has now disappeared but at the time of the Dudleys at Witley Court everyone had servants or had been one at one time in their lives. During the reigns of Queen Victoria (1837-1901) and of her son Edward VII (1901-10) - which nicely spans the Dudley Era at the Court rich families employed, in some cases hundreds of people to serve the great house and the family. Witley Court was only one of several homes the Dudleys owned and would not be used all the year round, but still many servants and staff were employed to keep the grounds, the gardens and the house in the best condition in readiness for the arrival of the family, their relatives and guests.

The magnificent portico entrance to Witley Court:-courtesy of English Heritage©

The same view of the entrance portico in 2012- notice the blocked up windows which formed part of the outer wall of the ballroom. The windows in this room on the other side looked out onto the terrace and the Flora fountain: JRH©

In 1891 the National Census gives us an idea of just how many people were employed as servants at this time. It states that there were almost two million indoor servants alone, including 100,000 children under the age of fifteen.

Most families treated their servants with respect and often affection; they were the great local employers. For many miles around Witley the local people were either employed in agriculture, and many of the farms were owned by the Dudleys or worked at the Court in one role or another, some outside and some indoors. Without the great houses many people would have been poverty-stricken and life would have been hard and cruel.

Royal Worcester made a moustache cup and saucer with a view of Witley in print in 1885:- courtesy of Royal Worcester Archives©

Life at Witley Court would have been run on the lines of most of the great aristocratic family homes of the time, and the Industrial Revolution in which the Dudleys played a major role had created many new rich industrialists who wished to emulate the lives and the great houses of such families as the 'Dudleys.'

Royal Worcester Archives have this photograph of a leather card case with a view of Witley Court from about 1830: courtesy of Royal Worcester Archives©

In looking for Census returns to show who lived and worked at the Court, this has proved quite difficult as the Dudley family were never at Witley Court for long periods of time, and unusually in the spring in March and April when a Census would be taken.

For the Census returns for 1881, 1901 and 1911 the family do not appear to be in residence. They were not at *Himley Hall*, which had been their main residence in the Midlands until the mining and industrial works in its vicinity made the Hall almost uninhabitable.

Their London residence at 100 Park Lane at '*Dudley House'* again proved difficult to find information for. The family when using this residence would have gone for the London season which did not take place until after Easter for three months when most aristocratic families descended on the capital.

The Dudleys of course owned many different homes, mainly in Scotland, Ireland and Wales and during the time of the census they may also have been abroad.

In 1911, for example, the Earl and Countess of Dudley as reported in *The Times* for the 4th March were retiring from their post as the *Governor General of Australia* in the summer, so the Dudleys must have been still in Australia when this particular census was taken.

In March 1901 the Earl is reported as being abroad when his agent was bidding for a Gainsborough portrait, so again was more than likely out of the country when this census was taken.

I have therefore included here the 1891 Census which gives us an idea of the staff who was at the Court at this time. It must be remembered that on special occasions such as the Earl of Dudley's 21ˢᵗ Celebrations or other important events when the Court was the centre of great festivities and entertainment, the staff would have doubled or even trebled in size.

The parterre gardens in about 1891 with the Flora Fountain in the background

Civil Parish of Great Witley	Census: RG12/2321	1891				
Name of House	Name and Surname	Relation to Head of Family	Condition as to marriage	Age last Birthday	Profession or Occupation	Where Born
Worcester Lodge	Edwin Cook	Head	M	60	Carpenter(retired)	Great Malvern
	Sarah Cook	Wife	M	56		Great Witley
	Ada Knowles	Niece		12	Scholar	Shrawley
	Martin Grissell	Boarder	S	21	Blacksmith	Martin Hussingtree
Witley Court Stable	EdwardBrown	Head	M	49	Head Coachman	Elanden Suffolk
	Rhoda Brown	Wife	M	38		Fevesham Kent
	Benjamin Turley		M	33	Groom Coachman	London Middlesex
	Walter Dunlop	Groom	S	16	Groom Servant	Great Witley
	George Asher	Servant	S	36	Groom Servant	Bedford
	James Edwards	Servant	S	28	Groom Servant	Upper Ottery Devon
	George Box	Servant	S	22	Groom Servant	Stourbridge
	George Hooler	Servant	S	25	Groom Servant	Neston Cheshire
	Eliza Neath	Servant	M	43	Servant	Dudley
	Charles Willis	Servant	S	25	Groom Servant	Tiverton Devon
	Charles Peckenham	Servant	S	31	Groom Servant	London
	Francis Evans	Servant	S	21	Groom Servant	Tedstone Hereford
Witley Court	Georgina Ward	Mother	Widow	43	Living on own means	Brighton
	Edith Ward	Sister	Single	18	Living on own means	Black Mount Argyllshire
	Reginald Ward	Brother	Single	16	School boy	London
	Gerald Ward	Brother	Single	12	Schoolboy	Witley Court
	Helen B. Forbes	Cousin	Single	21	Living on own means	London
	Mabel Forbes	Cousin	Single	20	Living on own means	London
	Marie Aeschliman	Visitor	Single	58	Governess	Switzerland
	Lord Annaly	Visitor	Married	34	Captain in the Scots Guards	Kingstown West Indies

53

Alfred Payne	Visitor	Married	41	J.P. Co Salop	Kinnerley, Salop
Kate Manger	Servant	Widow	48	Housekeeper	Marylebone, London
Jane Walker	Servant	Single	33	Cook-Servant	Wesley, Lanarkshire
Annie Edwards	Servant	Single	30	Ladies Made	HagleyWorcestershire
Mary Fayter	Servant	Single	38	Ladies Maid	Otter St..Mary Devonshire
Marie Strohacker	Servant	Single	32	Ladies Maid	Switzerland
Amelia Thompson	Servant	Single	26	Ladies Maid	Marylebone London
Christina Bethune	Servant	Single	29	Ladies Maid	Dyke Morayshire
Harriet Wells	Servant	Single	34	Housemaid	Barford Warwickshire
Mary Trimmer	Servant	Single	27	Housemaid	Thornton Buckinghamshire
Elizabeth Walker	Servant	Single	34	Housemaid	Himley Staffordshire
Elizabeth Goodman	Servant	Single	24	Housemaid	Stanford Worcestershire
Louisa Hughes	Servant	Single	30	Housemaid	Wall Heath Staffordshire
Susan Buchanan	Servant	Single	19	Housemaid	Spitalfield Dunkeld
Emily Bythway	Servant	Single	26	Kitche maid	Bitterley Shropshire
Florence Etches	Servant	Single	18	Kitchenmaid	Bampton Oxfordshire
Eunice Burcham	Servant	Single	19	Kitche maid	Ebbe Vale Monmouthshire
Clara Footman	Servant	Single	17	Stillroom Maid	Little Witley Worcestershire
Marjorie McKenzi	Servant	Single	30	Stillroom Maid	Murthly Perthshire
Caroline Gray	Servant	Single	42	Laundrymaid	Knockard Rossshire
Jane Aheron	Servant	Single	23	Laundrymaid	Dublin Ireland
Annie Merritt	Servant	Single	21	Laundrymaid	Whatley Oxfordshire
Charlotte Richards	Servant	Single	22	Laundrymaid	Shifnal Shropshire
Edith Shikman	Servant	Single	19	Laundrymaid	Wall Heath Staffordshire
Walter Wood	Servant	Single	29	Under Butler	Rackenford Devon
Charles Harrow	Servant	Married	27	Brass Finisher	St. Pancras London
John Skinner	Servant	Single	27	Footman	Bristol Gloucester
John Bennett	Servant	Single	27	Footman	Tomich Invernessshire

	John Bole	Servant	Single	24	Footman	Ancrain Scotland
	George Roberts	Servant	Single	24	Footman	Hilchen Herefordshire
	Henry Tipton	Servant	Single	27	Usher	Broadstone Shropshire
	James Dunlop	Servant	Single	20	Footman	Great Witley Worc
	Josiah Fuller	Servant	Single	32	Groom of Chambers	Cowston Norfolk
	William Clifford	Servant	Married	53	Butler	Newbury Berkshire
Gardiner's House	John Austin	Head	Married	46	Gardiner	Ledbury
	Clarinda Austin	Wife	Married	43		Kent, Canterbury
	George Austin	Son	Single	15	Clerk in Estate Office	Long Ashton Somerset
	Herbert Austin	Son	Single	13	Scholar	" "
	Edith Austin	Daughter	Single	11	Scholar	" "
	William Austin	Son	Single	10	Scholar	" "
	Horace Austin	Son	Single	8	Scholar	" "
	Francis E. Austin	Son	Single	5	Scholar	Great Witley, Worcs
	Cora Austin	Daughter	Single	2		Great Witley, Worcs
	Rebecca Jones	Servant	Single	21	Mothers Help	Holt, Worcs
Gardiners Bothy	Robert Hasbech	Head	Single	27	Gardiner	Yorkshire Croft
	Thomas Hall		Single	26	Gardiner	Bedale Yorks
	Ginge Carville		Single	27	Gardiner	Kent
	Thomas Webb		Single	22	Gardiner	Wiltshire Easton Grey
80 Witley Park	Thomas Hogg	Head	Married	49	Forester	Scotland
	Agnes Hogg	Wife	Married	50		Scotland
	Janet Hogg	Daughter	Single	22	Nurse	Leominster, Heref
	Jane Hogg	Daughter	Single	17		Leominster, Heref
	Lucy Hogg	Daughter	Single	10		Leominster, Heref
	Isabella Hogg	Daughter	Single	6		Staffordshire Cannock
79 Witley Park	William Lawley	Head	Married	59	Game Keeper	Kingswinford
	Joseph	Son	Married	29	Servant - Butler	St.Mary's

	Lawley					Kidderminster
	John Seale	Head	Married	59	Game Keeper	Norfolk Narborough
	Susan Seale	Niece	Married	52		Norfolk
	Edith		Single	25		Shrawley, Worcs

Thanks to Mrs Sue Campbell for researching this census and for correcting where needed the final copy.

This view is of the South Portico by John Nash. It is interesting to note the windows in the upper storey which are not decorated. They would have been out of sight when the roof was in place and were presumably for servants' rooms, high up in the roof of the Court:-JRH©

The Entrance Hall at Witley Court:-courtesy of English Heritage©

The same view in 2012:-JRH©

Lots of Wonderful things! - Some of the furnishings that
were for sale in the 1938 Witley Court Sale

Lot 337: 1938 Witley Court Sales Catalogue: A Louis XVI style Boulle cabinet: - courtesy of the Worcestershire Archive and Archaeology Service©

Lot 576: A 16th Century Florentine carved and gilt Cassone, having a tall raised back with ornamental and painted frieze and cornice, moulded and shaped lid with carved scale borders, floral and foliated side pillars, and massive claw feet, the raised back and front having painting, on the panels with battle and processional scenes, and the side panels painted with figures of saints.

Lot 343: A Louis XVI style Boulle Side Table, with massive and finely chased ormolu mounts, and having a shaped front fitted three drawers on reeded shaped supports.

Lot 581: An 18ᵗʰ Century Italian walnut and inlaid cabinet, having a shaped cornice with carved and gilt coronet and trophy centrepiece.

Lot 582: An 18ᵗʰ Century rare Marquetry and Boulle Flemish Cabinet, with an exquisite alcove interior, having mirror panels, ebonised and tortoiseshell Corinthian columns, the exterior fitted with ten drawers and centre door, richly mounted in gilt bronze and supported by two carved and draped figures on platform base with raised back.

The entrance portico on the north side of the Court with the French Classic urn shaped vase covered with figures, cupids gathering corn by Eugene Cornu:- courtesy of English Heritage©

Lot 324

Lot 325

Lot 325: 16th C. Beauvais Tapestry Screen, woven with floral arched panel enclosing a figure of a youth, seated on a pedestal with a dog and frames in a gilt wood Cheval stand, richly carved with mask figure surmounts, trophies, scrolls etc. Courtesy of Worcestershire Archive and Archaeology Service©

Lot 579   Lot 580

Lot 787

Lot 794

Lot 788

Lot 808

Lot 808: A pair of important French classic Urn shape vases, carved with figures, cupids, gathering corn the bowls carved in heavy relief, with flowers, fruit and foliage and having square bases by Eugene Cornu also the rough marble shaped pedestals. (These urns stood under the portico on the north side of the Court)

Lot: 787: Talia – Comedy

Lot: 788: Clio – History

Lot: 794 Euterpe – Lyric Poetry

Lot 579: A finely sculptured bronze group of a Herculean Figure carrying a bearded man, who is holding a statuette and leading a child, also the black marble square pedestal base (total height 5' 9")

Lot: 580: A finely sculptured bronze classical figure of a Sleeping Woman seated, also the black rectangular pedestal (total height 5' 3"):- These lots taken from the 1938 Sales Catalogue at Witley Court are by courtesy of Worcestershire Archive and Archaeology Service©

One of the main fireplaces in Witley Court which were being offered for sale: courtesy of the Worcestershire Archive and Archaeology Service©

The remains of one of the fireplaces which can still be seen in 2012- notice the bell pull device on either side of the chimney breast:-JRH©

It seems painfully sad, that although the fire in the autumn of 1937, caused a great deal of destruction, and because the house was not adequately insured the owner Sir Herbert Smith decided to cut his losses and just sell everything, even though it meant ripping the Court apart. Here is a list of what was for sale apart from the furniture and fittings in the Court:

'Special attention is called to –

The fine Mantelpieces throughout the mansion, by Flaxman and others, with massive set-in dog grates.

The ivory door knobs and door furniture. Fine oak panelled or mahogany and other doors.

The magnificent principal staircase, with wide treads and easy risers and finely designed wrought iron balustrading thereto.

The black and white polished granite flagging. The fine oak floors.

An interesting seventeenth century secondary staircase (from the original house) with finely turned balusters, newels etc.

A number of wrought iron gates and window grilles.

Numberless other fittings, masses of carved and other dressed stonework, flagging, slates, bricks, joists, iron lead work and other first-class materials.'

———————————————————————————

Lot 970

Lot 970: Extremely fine Kirman Carpet containing the heads and figures of 108 former Shahs of
Persia woven and signed by Mohammed Ibn Djafar in Kirman:- courtesy of Worcestershire Archive
and Archaeology Service© (This may not have been part of the Dudley Collection- as Sir Herbert
Smith who bought the Court after the Dudleys collected some superb and very rare carpets.)

In the Sale were included some of the many fine marble mantelpieces which could be found throughout the Court by Flaxman and others, with their massive set in dog grates:- courtesy of English Heritage©

Lot 809

Lot 803

Lot 801

Lot 796

Lot: 809: A rectangular panel sculptured in heavy relief with classical figures, cupids and emblems.

Lot 803 – 'I'm first Sir!' A large group of Two Newspaper Boys by G. Focardi, London 1880, also the wooden pedestal.

Lot 801: A classical nude female figure with snake entwining around her foot, by L. Macdonald, 1848, also the massive red marble pedestal.

Lot 796: A pair of a large massive group with dogs and a cherub by Auguste Lechesne 1853 with red marble pedestals.

The Dining Room at Witley Court:-courtesy of English Heritage©

The Service Bells

A system of bells in the servants' hall showed when and where service was needed and some elaborate codes were introduced to suit the individual needs of the house. Later came the speaking tube and then the telephone. The original system was invented about 1780 and meant that servants no longer had to loiter in corridors within earshot of the family. Most of the bells were electric, as in the case of Witley Court. The palace was on such a vast scale that this was necessary, even though electricity came late to the Court as Lady Dudley did not take to the newfangled electricity and liked to keep the old lamps and candles instead.

Evidence of the later bell system at the Court can still be seen today. Mr Jason Fisher has kindly carried out some study on the bell system and his findings are most interesting and shed new light on the life at the Court:

'The bell systems of these old houses have always interested me, and I personally think it's really fascinating that at Witley, parts of the bell systems are still to be found in situ and have survived. Here at Witley Court, this would have been a mechanical system using tensioned copper wire and bell cranks (not Pulleys) to direct the wires behind plaster mouldings etc...The copper wires were always run in small zinc tubes from the bell pull

which would have been positioned beside the fireplaces – because the wires had to run up to the roof which meant they could be run up the chimneys. Below is an example of just such a system alongside the fireplace.'

This one is excellent...the tubing is still in place stapled to the chimney. This would have carried the operating wire down to the bell pull, the drum of which is still attached to the wall.

This image is a type of mechanism which does not actually use a bell pull as such, but rather an ornate handle which turns inside the drum. A sharp turn of the handle causes the wire to be pulled.

Here you can see the various wires dangling from a wooden box frame containing bell cranks for the various apartments.'

This picture shows one of the cranks in place with the bell wire still attached, all hidden behind a wooden inspection plate: courtesy of Jason Fisher©

A view of the entrance hall to Witley Court with a magnificent staircase in the distance:-courtesy of English Heritage©

The area where the magnificent staircase once stood. The line on the wall shows where it once was sited. The fine decorative plasterwork gives an idea of the splendour which once could be seen here:-JRH©

A faint imprint of faded wallpaper in the Red Room and some decorative work from the staircase area in 2012:-JRH©

The line of the staircase and the decorative plasterwork in 2012:- JRH©

Behind the Scenes at the Court

On a tour behind the scenes at Witley Court one can still even now, over 72 years since the Court was sold and abandoned see clues showing what life was like in this vast Victorian palace.

Here is what is left of the enormous coal fired boilers which provided heat for the Court:

The boilers which once helped to heat and power Witley Court: courtesy of Jason Fisher©

The *'Witley Court Boiler'* was said to have been invented by G. Westland the Head Gardener. This is described in *the Gardeners' Chronicle of 1872* and was manufactured by Jones & Rowe and tested at Northwick Park in Worcester. The boiler was versatile and rather like a modern stove burning refuse, wood, coal and coke.

The reconstructed bell tower over the stable block with the tiled courtyard which once rang with the sound of horses hooves and carriages:-JRH©

The entrance from the stables with the reconstructed bell tower:-JRH©

The rear of the Servants' quarters and also including the Nursery areas. Once ringing with the sounds of voices and laughter- today eerily silent: -JRH©

Part of the Kitchen range at Witley Court where once the sumptuous banquets fit for Princes and Kings were prepared:-JRH©

Once the visiting grooms and carriage drivers would have warmed themselves while waiting for their masters to call them:-JRH©

Some of the decorative ironwork still in place at the Court probably made in the Dudley's own foundries in the Black Country:-JRH©

Life Below Stairs

A painting of a typical Victorian serving girl: - courtesy of Sir William Ripley Bt©

There was at the height of Witley Court's time, some cold water plumbing but no hot water systems as such. For safety and economy reasons few of the many fireplaces at Witley Court were left alight overnight. At the Court there would have been a 'nightsman,' whose role, when everyone else was asleep was to clean the boots and trim the wicks on the many candles and oil lamps, as electricity was not installed at the Court until the twentieth century. Coal and wood had to be brought in to prepare for the coming day, and the kitchen fires had to be lit early to prepare for breakfast for the staff in the kitchen areas and in the winter in the main rooms the family would later be using. Many of the staff would have been up well before dawn.

Those who rose first would be scullery maids, those servants both men and women, boys and girls who were at the lowest of the social standing- they would be expected to be up and cleaning the fireplaces, heating the water and laying up breakfast for the other servants who would rise around 7.00 a.m. The maids and male servants would now have to prepare the trays and breakfast in the dining room for the family.

The roles of the male servants were very different from the female roles and it is interesting to see the roles in action at an enormous house such as Witley Court. There were the permanent staff many of whom lived-in, and many brought from a distance rather than employing local people who may gossip about the goings-on in the 'big house'. In terms of Witley Court, this was one of several other houses that the family owned and lived in and so always had a permanent staff both in the house and in the grounds. At certain times of the year, such as the 'London Season' or when the family were on holiday in Scotland, Ireland or abroad as in the case of the Dudleys - many of the servants would go with their households to the different locations leaving a 'skeleton staff behind.' At other times, temporary staff would be employed as when the family were all at home and they entertained and had guests and relatives staying at the Court. On the important occasions such as the family birthday celebrations and when Royalty or other important guests stayed for the weekend parties, then the house would be full of both full-time and temporary staff. In the case of Witley Court this could amount to hundreds of people being brought in to ensure that everything went smoothly for the family and their guests.

The Work of the Male Servants:

Probably the most important male servant employed at Witley Court was for outside the Coachman and his staff and inside the Court the Butler would rule. His role was an ancient one, and his title derives from the Old French '*bouteillier,*' meaning a servant.

The butler had several important roles, and the choice of a butler had to be undertaken very carefully as he would be a man of integrity and pride, a man who could command and issue orders effectively to the other staff and hold a great respect for the family he was employed by.

One of his roles was to oversee the wine cellar, and in a mansion such as Witley Court this was a very specialised task, requiring knowledge of wine, brandy, liquors and the other requirements for the day's drinks and particularly the specialist choices required for fine dinner parties and other such events. He would be skilled at bottling and decanting of wine as well as in its general care. If beer was brewed, the task of managing it also fell to his lot. Besides looking after the wine cellar the butler was in charge of the family plate, which in the case of the Dudleys was very extensive and very valuable and needed to be at all times watched carefully and treated with the utmost care- in fact the butler's rooms were always sited close to the family silver, which was often kept in elaborate safes with only the butler having the key.

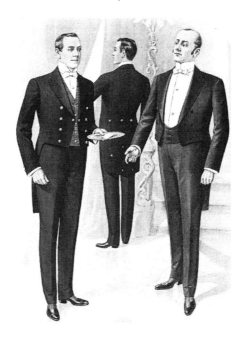

Together with the footman, and there would have been several at Witley Court, the butler was expected to wait at table, and the overall responsibility for the arrangements rested with him. It was he who announced in the drawing room to the assembled guests that all was ready.

Besides the butler, the Dudleys would have employed several footmen, and they probably more than any other servant were regarded as conspicuous symbols of wealth.

Royal liverymen- the Dudleys would have had equally grand uniforms for their footmen and liverymen.

That this was so is clear from the elaborate and expensive liveries that they wore, both inside and outside the house. None of the women servants could compete with this display. The cost of the expensive livery was covered by the employers and this was always expected to be kept in the very best condition at all times - the footman represented the family in public and their role was clearly defined.

When the footman was performing his public duties, either in the dining room, drawing and sitting rooms or the hall, the footman observed Mrs Beeton, should be '*attentive to all...(but) obtrusive to none.*' He was expected to move effortlessly and silently, speaking to no one unless spoken to, deaf to all conversation and with shoes that did not commit the 'abomination' of creaking or squeaking.

It was part of the footman's responsibility also to ensure that all the footwear of the family was kept in peak condition as well as the shoes of their guests. At Witley Court, being on such a large scale, there would have been several under-footmen and boys to complete these tasks. At Witley there was a specific 'lampman' employed for the enormous task of cleaning, trimming and filling the oil lamps of which there would have been several hundred at Witley Court- electricity was not introduced at the Court until after the Dudleys had left.

The Work of Female Servants:

At Witley Court as in other great country houses in Victorian and Edwardian times, footmen were expected to move silently and unobtrusively around the house, but housemaids were meant to be invisible and had to have all their cleaning jobs completed either before the family were up in the mornings or while they were absent.

Housemaids were obliged to be up very early. Mrs Beeton commented: '*The housemaid who studies her own ease will certainly be at her work by six o'clock in the summer, and probably, half-past six in the winter months, having spent a reasonable time in her own chamber in dressing. Other than that would, probably, be an unnecessary waste of coals and candle in winter.'*

Mrs Beeton's Book of Household Management

One of the first tasks the housemaids had to carry out would have been to make sure all was ready in the servants' hall for the other servants when they came down and that the breakfast table was laid and the water heated.

The housemaid would open the downstairs shutters and clean out the fireplaces which could be relaid ready to light when needed. Witley Court was said to have used up to fifty tons of coal a day, especially in the winter and if the family were at home, as they often spent Christmas here in Worcestershire.

It was only by means of a strict routine that the work of keeping the house clean could be achieved. Every day was timetabled strictly by the housekeeper, so that all her staff would know exactly what was required of them. Much had to be done before the family were up and about in the house.

Many housemaids and ladies maids came from the ranks of dressmaker's assistants, since sewing together with a knowledge of hairdressing were essential skills. The lady's maid would be expected to help her mistress to dress and undress and to care for her hair and her wardrobe.

A typical Victorian parlourmaid or lady's maid from the time of Witley Court

The Housekeeper would have had her own room at Witley Court and was responsible for the running of the household.

Another important member of the staff was of course the cook, and good cooks were often in short supply and much in demand by the larger houses. The role of the cook can be summarised in *The Servant's Practical Guide* which commented: *'some ladies stand much in awe of their cooks, knowing that those who consider themselves thoroughly experienced will not brook fault-finding, or interference with their manner of cooking and give notice to leave on the smallest pretext. Thus, when ladies obtain a really good cook, they deal with her delicately, and are inclined to let her have her own way with the regard to serving the dinner.'*

The busy times for the cook were in the morning and the early evening. In the morning the family would be served breakfast, some in the dining room while others preferred to have trays sent to their rooms. The cook would also meet with the mistress of the house to discuss the menus for the day or for a special occasion for the many important guests who would be dining at the Court. Soups had to be prepared and other foods for the following day; pastries, jellies and other delicacies were to be made ready for the evening and luncheon had to be cooked and as in the case of Witley enormous hampers to be made ready to serve those who were going hunting or shooting or even for a family picnic on some part of the estate or garden during the day.

From five until at least ten in the evening was the time of the greatest activity when the huge dinners would be served. This is when the nerves of the staff were at their most tense. In the words of *The Servant's Practical Guide*, *'perfect silence is enjoined save when an order is given concerning the work in hand.'* As in a modern hotel kitchen, tempers would have flared as hot food must be served at the exact time or it would spoil. After dinner had been served, the cook's work for the day was done, but for the scullery maids and kitchen maids, everything had to be cleared away before the morning tasks started all over again. Washing up alone was a formidable task, as at Witley Court dinner may have involved serving a whole crowd of guests and visitors and their staff had to be fed as well as the Court's staff themselves. After everyone had eaten, everything had to be left clean and tidy before the final staff were allowed to retire to bed.

A large Victorian palace such as Witley Court created large volumes of laundry - at Witley the laundry was done mostly 'in-house' with laundry staff being employed on a permanent basis when the family were in residence. In earlier times hedges of lavender and rosemary were even grown, for the specific purpose of imparting a pleasant smell to the drying clothes hung on them. Laundry maids tended to be an independent group and not always under the control of the housekeeper herself. Their proximity, as at Witley Court, to the grooms and the stable lads were often considered a problem and walls were built to keep them separate. At Packenhall in Ireland the laundry was linked to the drying grounds by an underground passage (installed in the 1840s), which ran the length of the stables and reduced the chance of laundry maids meeting stable lads.

The Dinner Party

One of the many fine bedrooms at Witley Court- at one time several score of guests could be staying at the Court and these would bring their own retinue of servants who must also be housed:- courtesy of English Heritage©

Dinner was the main meal of the day in the Victorian household and often took place as early at 6.30 or 7p.m. and could last for several hours. In a house such as Witley Court or when they were in London at *Dudley House* or *Carlton Place* it would have been customary to always dress for dinner - full length evening dress for the ladies and white tie for the gentlemen (dinner jackets were not completely accepted until after 1900).

Before dinner drinks would be served to give the family and the guests time to get together to socialise before being given set places at the dinner table - usually the Countess would have already decided who would be sitting next to whom and the relevant place cards put in place. She would also decide on the menu for that particular evening which would have been printed carefully on decorative menu cards.

Dinner was always, a formal meal, and the best silver and crystal were brought out for the occasion. The silver was of course a sign of status and the Dudleys had many valuable and beautiful pieces of silverware to display at table. The main dining room would have been used for dinner but the ballroom would have been used for special occasions such as the weekend parties and particularly when important guests and visitors were in residence at the Court. The evenings that the Prince of Wales was in attendance must have been spectacular with the chandeliers in the main ballroom being lit, reflecting the gold gilt on the walls and the silverware and crystal laid out on the table. Grace was usually said at the start of the meal and often the ladies were presented beforehand with exotic flowers to wear for the meal. Flowers would also have been displayed on the tables alongside such fine articles as decorative salt cellars and other items of fine silver or gold.

The Countess would have discussed the menu for each meal carefully with the cook and with the housekeeper and butler who would need to decide what staff they needed to serve at table and to help in the kitchens. For great events, many staff would be drafted in from the local area to help with this. Often the sources for menus were *Mrs Beeton's Household Management (1861)* or *Francatelli's Cook's Guide (1862)*. When Prince Albert, Princess Alexandra and the many important guests who would have been invited alongside the royal party were due to stay at the Court - weeks before the staff of the relevant parties would have been consulted as to the favourite choices of the various guests and their particular likes and dislikes, so that there would be no problems at the dinner table itself.

Dinner usually consisted of five or six courses and this could be extended to nine or even ten. The Earl or his Butler would carve the meat, and vegetables were handed separately to each diner. Footmen waited at table, but any available servant could be called in to help. Resident male guests may be served by their own valets - of course the footmen would be in uniform and be as unobtrusive as possible - to wait on table to see that no glass had been emptied and then not refilled, and to be silent at all times and not to listen to conversation or to join in unless consulted directly.

After dinner, the ladies would withdraw to an adjoining drawing room for tea and coffee and liqueurs, leaving the men alone to enjoy fruit, nuts, port, brandy and cigars. The decanters were passed from diner to diner and always from the left hand side.

The servants were expected to help both at the table and in the kitchens and also with the massive task of clearing away after the guests had retired which could be many hours later. Of course everyone had to be up in the morning at the same time as usual, as no 'lie-ins' were ever allowed. In most houses there were compensating periods of quiet when the family were away and even in some cases an extra bonus to the wage packet or gift for the servants to say 'thank you' after a particular busy period in the house.

At Witley Court if the family were in residence for Christmas, there was always a massive Christmas tree which was covered with jewels. When the guests left after the weekend they were asked to select a gift from the tree.

The Christmas Tree at Witley Court in 1913: courtesy of Ray Jones©

In the Country- Shooting Parties and Royalty

After the end of the London season usually in August, the wealthy families returned to their estates and there followed several months devoted to country business, sports and pleasure.

Local seasons were arranged around different hunts, point-to-points, stock sales and sometimes the various families had arranged to spend time in such Spa towns as Cheltenham or Bath and at nearby Malvern Spa and Droitwich Spa which was particularly popular.

The shooting parties and hunting were a major part of the sporting autumn and winter calendars, with music, rich dining and cards in the evenings. Weekend parties became very popular indeed and when Prince Albert the later Edward VIIth bought Sandringham in the 1860s, he enjoyed all the activities of the country and liked nothing better than travelling around the homes and estates of his rich friends enjoying their lavish hospitality. The Prince visited Witley Court on various occasions before he became King. After this time he was preoccupied with affairs of state, but still enjoyed his social life to the full.

Edward Prince of Wales was the ruler of this aristocratic and wealthy world, and he liked to control proceedings precisely. Punctuality was the order of the day and in many homes where he was due to stay the clocks were moved 30 minutes ahead to ensure no one was late for the Prince.

Guests could travel by rail in special coaches, where the family carriages would meet them and convey them to Witley Court. The Prince himself liked to allocate rooms. His rooms overlooked the splendid Flora Fountain on the east side of the Court.

The Flora Fountain at Witley Court: - courtesy of the Worcestershire Archive and Archaeology Service© & in 2011:-JRH©

Witley Court Gardens in their full glory:-courtesy of Ray Jones (www.surfworcester.co.uk) (c)

PART OF FOUNTAIN AT WITTY COURT, WORCESTERSHIRE.

Designed by Mr. W. A. Nesfield; Executed by Mr. Jas. Forsyth, and Others.

Engraving from the Builder from February 19th 1860:-courtesy of Worcester Library©

The splendid Forsyth font in Witley Church: - JRH©

Engraving of Witley Court: - courtesy Worcestershire Archives and Archaeology Service©

The Fallow Deer at Charlecote in Warwickshire, similar to those at Witley Court: JRH©

The two bronze fighting lions by A. Cain 1878: courtesy of the 1938 Sales Catalogue and the
Worcestershire Archive and Archaeology Service©

The magnificent Ballroom at Witley Court: - courtesy of English Heritage©

The Entrance Hall at Witley Court: - courtesy of English Heritage©

The interior of St Michael and All Angels at Witley Court showing the magnificent organ in its
Baroque setting: - by courtesy of the Parochial Church Council and Parishioners: - JRH©

Joshua Price 'Baptism of Christ from St Michael and All Angels at Witley: - courtesy of the Parochial Church Council and Parishioners: - JRH©

Detail from Joshua Price's window at Witley Court: courtesy of the Parochial Church Council©

The parterre gardens and the Flora Fountain in April 2011- the beds are filled with tulips:-JRH©

Some of the stunning varieties of rhododendrons which have been replanted at Witley Court by English Heritage: - JRH©

Teapot which was a duplicate for the Earl and Countess's Wedding Gift in the 1870s:-courtesy of the Royal Worcester Porcelain Archives©

The Stourport and Worcester Lodges at Witley Court:-courtesy of the Worcestershire Archive and Archaeology Service & JRH©

Auguste Cain's Bronze lions which once stood on the terrace at Witley Court, now on the entrance gates to Harlaxton Hall – Lincolnshire©

Dudley House at 100 Park Lane-London:-courtesy of English Heritage©

Part of a set of China Dinner Service displaying the Dudley Coat of Arms and Earl and Countess Wedding gift from Royal Worcester Porcelain:- courtesy of Royal Worcester Porcelain©

The visit to Witley Court of Prince Albert and Princess Alexandra :-courtesy of Royal Worcester Porcelain©

Shooting party at Witley Court showing the First Earl and Prince Albert:- courtesy of Royal Worcester Porcelain©

The Bassano portrait of Georgina Elizabeth Ward c.1880s - Countess of Dudley:-courtesy of the National Portrait Gallery in London©

An early photograph of Witley Court c.1860-1900:-courtesy of Ray Jones (@) – www-surfworcester.co.uk

RUSSELL & SONS

29 UNION ROAD,   LONDON, N.W. &

TUFNELL PARK,   EAST St, CHICHESTER.

PHOTOGRAPHERS TO THE ROYAL FAMILY.

Georgina Countess of Dudley with four of her children: - courtesy of Ray Jones©

The Christmas tree in the splendid ballroom of Witley Court c.1913:- courtesy of Ray Jones©

Chapter Three - The Gardens and the Fountains

Witley Court: courtesy of Olive and Bernard Poultney of 'Westwood'©

Witley Court and the Church are situated on the far side of a valley into which was created the Front Pool, which was originally formed in the 18th century by damming a stream. Visitors to the Court would have once reached the house by a causeway across the lake linked to the mansion via a driveway to the front of the north portico.

The Royal Horticultural Society have two interesting articles on Witley Court, the first from the *Journal of Horticulture and Cottage Gardener* for January 1873 and one from *The Gardeners' Chronicle* for October 15th 1881 which give an interesting insight into the gardens and parkland at Witley Court in the time of the Dudleys. The Court then was one of the finest Victorian palaces in the country.

The South front view of the Court with partially restored gardens in 2011:- JRH©

Taking notes from *The Gardeners' Chronicle* we can get an interesting insight into the gardens and their layout at this particular time in the history of the Court:

'The well-known seat of the Earl of Dudley and one of the finest palatial residences in England, stands upon an eminence, and overlooks the most complete geometrical gardens in the kingdom, of well-proportions, and surrounded by a park richly diversified by Nature in its formation and abounding in giant Oaks, and other noble trees situated in one of the most picturesque districts in Worcestershire, about 6 miles from Stourport, the drive being of the most pleasant description, the air bracing, and the woodland scenery refreshing in the extreme. From the main road to the entrance, which is but a short walk, there are many evidences of rural sublimity and quiet industry, but once you enter the lodge gates the attractions grow too numerous for one to contemplate much for the details of rural life.'

The Worcester Lodge, taken from the East Drive Entrance. This lodge was the main entrance for the family and visitors. *The Stourport Lodge* at the opposite end of the drive was used by estate staff and tradesmen: Courtesy of the 1938 Sales Catalogue – Worcestershire Archive and Archaeology Service©

'The avenue calls for no special comment beyond the mention of its fine trees and the rich verdure upon either side. The house, an immense pile, has been remodelled and enlarged, and the principal front on the south side, containing the largest apartments, possesses a fine elevation and commands extensive views of the surrounding country.

The *'Stourport Lodge'* in 2011:- JRH© - The original lodges were replaced in 1888 by the existing lodges in the French Second Empire style, designed by *Henry Rowe of Worcester.*

From the terrace (south and east) splendid views of the gardens and park are obtained, but of course the chief attractions are the fountains, the principle of which is the group of Perseus and Andromeda (on the south front) the largest piece of sculpture in Europe. The figures are 26 feet high from the water line, and 24 feet in diameter at its octagon base: were designed by Nesfield, and executed by Forsyth in Portland Stone. The legend according to Ovid is that as Perseus was passing the territories of Libya he descried on the coast of Ethiopia the naked Andromeda chained to a rock, and exposed to the furies of the sea monster. Struck with the sight he raised himself in the air, riding on his flying horse, flew to the monster and slew it. For this he obtained the lady in marriage. He is represented in the act of his chivalrous rescue, mounted on the winged steed Pegasus. The water for supplying the fountain is brought from a reservoir a mile distant, to which it is forced by a steam-engine of 40-horse power, yielding an average supply of 5000 gallons a minute, the maximum being 10,000, capable of being kept eight hours a day with all the jets in full play, the centre one sending water up to a height of 120 feet. The cost of this waterworks and sculpture exceeded £20,000. This was figured in our volume for 1883, p.813.'

PART OF FOUNTAIN AT WITTY COURT, WORCESTERSHIRE.
Designed by Mr. W. A. Nesfield; Executed by Mr. Jas. Forsyth, and Others.

The illustration of the design for the fountain at Witley Court (called here Witty Court) from the 'Builder' for February 19th 1859: courtesy of Worcester Library©

The description of the *'Fountain at Witty Court'* in Worcester from the *'Builder'* is interesting and reads as follows:

'Very considerable works are being executed at Witty Court, for Lord Ward. The house is being improved and fitted up under the direction of Mr. Daukes, architect, and the grounds are being arranged and adorned by Mr. W. A. Nesfield. Forming part of the latter works is a basin, 180 feet by 120 feet, having in the centre a fountain of large size and cost, part of which we have engraved. The group represented, Perseus and Andromeda,

97

surmounts an octagon basement, 24 feet in diameter, on which are shells and dolphins throwing water, with vases at intervals. It was designed by Mr. Nesfield, and is being executed in Portland stone by Mr. Forsyth; Messrs. J. Geefs and A. Waagen having assisted in the modelling. The fountain will be 26 feet in height from the waterline, and will probably be completed in October next. Messrs. Easton and Co. are the engineers.

The Perseus and Andromeda Fountain at Witley Court:- courtesy of Bernard and Olive Poultney of 'Westwood'©

Mr. Wood of Worcester was the builder employed on the house. The Carton Pierre ornamentation for the ceilings and panelling of the rooms, which by the way, is elaborate, after the style of Louis XVI was by a Frenchman. Mr. Moxon is the painter and decorator.'

William Andrews Nesfield (1793-1881)

William Andrews Nesfield was a landscape gardener who was chosen by the first Earl Dudley to design the new gardens at Witley Court. Nesfield came to call this his *'monster work'.*

Nesfield was born in Lumley Park, County Durham. In 1808 after the death of his mother the family moved a few miles to Brancepeth, where his father became the rector of St. Brandon's Church. His stepmother was Marianne Mills of Willington Hall, whose nephew was the noted architect Anthony Salvin. William's younger sister married Salvin.

William Andrews Nesfield

After his education at Durham School, Nesfield joined the army and fought under the Duke of Wellington in Spain and at the Battle of Waterloo. He also served for two years in Canada. He retired in 1816 and took up a new career as a watercolour artist which earned the praise of John Ruskin.

While still exhibiting his work at the *Old Water Colour Society,* Nesfield began work as a professional landscape architect with the encouragement and support of Salvin. From the 1840s until his death he was responsible either singly or with his sons Arthur Markham and William Eden for no fewer than 259 commissions in the British Isles. His earlier military training gave him the ability to have the skill of map drawing, and this enabled him to design the intricate water features which were so much a part of the gardens he landscaped. His work included not just Witley Court but also Castle Howard where he refashioned the gardens and installed the Prince of Wales Fountain in the 1850s. At Oxon Hoath he was engaged by Admiral Sir Francis Geary, who was Nelson's mentor, to create formal gardens in the style of Capability Brown. The Oxon Hoath gardens are the only surviving unaltered parterre gardens in England.

Nesfield also worked in Kew Gardens, and at Treberfydd the Victorian mansion built by John Loughborough Pearson for the Raikes family in 1852.

Treberfydd by John Loughborough Pearson- 1852

Kinmel Hall, which was the third house to be built on the same site in North Wales, was designed by Nesfield's son, William Eden Nesfield. It was completed in the 1870s, and W. A. Nesfield was responsible for the adjoining 18 acres of walled gardens.

Kinmel Hall- designed by William Nesfield's son, William Eden Nesfield in 1870

'The Prince of Wales Fountain' at Castle Howard

James Forsyth (1826-1910)

James Forsyth was born in Kelso, Roxburghshire where the Earl of Dudley owned property and had a shooting lodge. The Earl invited James and his brother William to England where James worked with Nesfield on the gardens and the sculpture at Witley Court.

James lived in London and exhibited his work at the Royal Academy from the mid-1860s through to the 1880s. He specialised in religious works, in a classical vein, and also produced some genre work.

In the 1850s and 60s the Earl of Dudley spent an estimated £250,000 (c. £15,000,000 today) transforming Witley Court into a Victorian Italianate Palace. Besides sculpturing the enormous *Perseus and Andromeda* fountain, he also sculpted the beautiful and moving font in St. Michael's parish church with its superb crouching angels. In the Court itself, Forsyth was responsible for many of the marble fireplaces and other sculptures in the gardens.

James Forsyth's beautiful font in St. Michael's Parish Church: - JRH© (see colour plate)

James named one of his sons John Dudley Forsyth in honour of his patron at Witley Court, and another son he named James Nesfield in honour of William Nesfield with whom he worked so closely at Witley Court.

In the 1860s James was also working on a relief entitled *Christ Appearing to the Disciples* for St. Dionysius Parish Church at Market Harborough and another relief *The Ascension* intended for Trinity Hall, Cambridge.

In 1861 he began work on the Village Cross for West Derby, Liverpool, again working to William Nesfield's designs. It was completed in 1870. In 1862 he contributed the fine carving for the alabaster font in Lichfield Cathedral.

The marble font in Lichfield Cathedral: - courtesy of the Dean and Chapter of Lichfield Cathedral©

In 1861, James was living in London with his wife Eliza and his baby daughter Agnes, and at the time of the census, she was one month old. They lived at 8 Edward Street, Marylebone. Their happiness was however short - lived as in 1864, Agnes died and Joseph assuaged his grief by creating a memorial to her in Abney Park Cemetery. The very moving carving, shows Agnes's face on one side and a biblical scene on the reverse. His grief continued when in 1867 he lost his wife Eliza.

In spite of his loss, James threw himself into creating the ambitious fountain which was donated to the town of Dudley by the Earl of Dudley. The fountain is richly decorated with fruit and flowers and with figures representing Commerce, Industry, Agriculture and Mining. The lower basins were fed with water for horses and cattle, spouting from the mouths of seahorse and dolphins, while people could drink from the water flowing from the lions' heads.

The fountain was unveiled by the Countess of Dudley on October 17th 1867, followed by the presentation of a ceremonial goblet of water from which the Countess drank. It was presented to her by James Forsyth himself.

James Forsyth's Dudley Fountain©

No full inventory of James Forsyth's work has ever been compiled, but a beginning can be made by listing all the monuments attributed to him by Professor Pevsner and his informants in the *'Buildings of England'*. The list is certainly incomplete and in some details erroneous, because a certain amount of confusion occurs everywhere not only between James and his younger brother William, but also between him and his son, James Nesfield Forsyth, who was also a sculptor and a monumental mason.

We also know that James was responsible for much of the excellent work with *Salvin* at *Wells* and at *Cragside*, the Rothbury home of the armaments king, Lord Armstrong, namely the fine stone carvings in the dining room and the excellent wooden panelling in both dining rooms and the library.

Cragside, the Rothbury home of the 'Armaments King', Lord Armstrong:-courtesy of the National Trust©

FOUNTAIN AT WITLEY COURT

Forsyth's famous Perseus and Andromeda Fountain at Witley Court: - courtesy of Olive and Bernard Poultney of 'Westwood'©

By 1871, James had remarried. His wife's name was Annie, and the couple went on to have at least nine children.

In 1868, James worked with Nesfield on the restoration of the church of St. Mary, at Kings Walden in Hertfordshire; James provided a stone reredos, the organ case and a table tomb.

In 1880 he began to exhibit work at the Glasgow Institute of Fine Arts and by 1881, he was employing 18 men and 8 boys in his workshop. He also exhibited at the Royal Academy.

James died in 1910, leaving behind a huge legacy of work, but none has the personal pathos of the monument of his daughter Agnes.

James's final works for the Dudley family were the splendid table tombs in Worcester Cathedral to Lord Lyttleton and to the Earl of Dudley himself. The Earl was buried at Witley but his body was removed in 1953 to the magnificent tomb in the Cathedral.

The splendid tomb of the First Earl of Dudley. Designed by Sir Gilbert Scott and sculpted by Forsyth: - courtesy of the Dean and Chapter of Worcester Cathedral© This sculpture is labelled as being sculpted by James Forsyth- but the father or the son?

Lord Lyttelton by Forsyth. The brother-in law of Gladstone and ancestor of the present Viscount Cobham. As Lord Lieutenant of Worcester, he was with the Earl of Dudley instrumental in raising the funds for the 1874 Restoration: - courtesy of the Dean and Chapter of Worcester Cathedral©

William Forsyth-

The obituary notice on William Forsyth, James's brother, a much more modest figure than his elder brother, is ironically much fuller and more informative. It repeats the facts about his Scottish origin, his Edinburgh training and his early years in London, and then goes on to mention how he came to settle in Worcester.

'Mr Forsyth's settlement in Worcester resulted indirectly from his engagement, in conjunction with his brother James to execute the carving incidental to the restoration of Eastnor Church which was being carried out by Mr McCann of Malvern, under the direction of (later Sir) Gilbert Scott. The work gave so much satisfaction to the Somers family that Viscount Eastnor, as he then was (the father of Lady Henry Somerset and her sister the Duchess of Bedford) invited Mr Forsyth soon afterwards to take up residence at Eastnor Castle for the purpose of beautifying the splendid hall which is so much admired by visitors.'

Eastnor Castle

After his work at Eastnor, William returned to Worcester and established himself at 6, The Tything. During the next forty years he executed a large number of works for neighbouring churches. He also made a copy of his brother's pulpit in Worcester Cathedral for the church at *Shaw, Oldham*. He cut in salt some fantastical figures for Mr John Corbett the 'Worcestershire Salt King' and created the figures of *Spring* and *Winter* for his home at *Impney Hall* (later Chateau Impney) – (see author's book on both Chateau Impney and John Corbett- www.johnrichard.fast-page.org) He also produced many works for clients in other countries.

William Forsyth's statue of 'spring' or 'Flora' in front of Impney Hall (Chateau Impney):- JRH©

Ian Mantle in front of the sculpture of William's statue of 'Winter' at Chateau Impney

Chateau Impney built by John Corbett (1817-1901) the 'Worcestershire Salt King':-JRH©

'William was also responsible for the Hop Pickers frieze in Sansome Street, Worcester; a reredos at St. Peter's, Malvern, another at Besford and a third at St. John's Cradley; Pitchcroft gates, Worcester; a pulpit in Llanwarne, Herefordshire; some unspecified work at Madresfield Court, Hanley Hall and Church, and Battenhall Mount, Worcester, a bust of Joseph Wood and a staircase at Davenham, Malvern; and some unspecified work on the Edgar Tower and other parts of the Cathedral in Worcester.' - Transactions of the Worcestershire Archaeological Society-1984.

'The Hop Pickers' frieze in Sansome Street-Worcester: JRH©

The gates at Pitchcroft in Worcester: - JRH©

Details on the Pitchcroft Gates: JRH©

Forsyth's account book throws a great deal of light on the work and life of a monumental mason and woodcarver in a provincial city in the latter part of the nineteenth century. Most of the 'bread and butter' work apart from specific commissions came from providing headstones and memorials which appealed to the 'Victorian cult of death.' Forsyth constructed a vault at Solihull for over £600; a mural tablet for the Rt. Hon. Lord Norton cost nearly £120; a tomb for Mr Berrow cost £180; one for Mrs Holland of Rose Hill £230 - probably one of the most lucrative commissions was to provide a copy of the Worcester Cathedral pulpit for Mr Clegg of Shaw, near Oldham, who paid no less than £820 or equivalent to some £30,000 today.

The table tomb to Mr and Mrs Holland of Rose Hill, Worcester in Astwood Cemetery in Worcester- said to have cost £230:-JRH©

Another fine tomb to Thomas Rowley Hill and family of St. Catherine's Hill, Worcester-
the tomb is unnamed but is maybe from the Forsyth workshop:-JRH©

The pulpit in Worcester Cathedral, designed by Sir Gilbert Scott, sculpted by Forsyth and paid for by Lord Dudley: - courtesy of the Dean and Chapter of Worcester Cathedral©

_____

The Gardeners' Chronicle continues with its contemporary descriptions of the gardens in 1881.

'The garden is enclosed by an elaborate stone balustrade, and its beauty (as I have already stated) is enhanced by its well-balanced proportions. In looking at the garden there is a pleasing admixture of shrubs and trees, the two borders at the southern extremity flanking the garden upon either side being a recent addition in the shape of a mixture of shrubs and the taller kinds of flowers.

I will now proceed with the details and arrangement of the different styles of grouping plants adopted by Mr. Westland, with such good taste and effect. Approaching the terrace from the west side, a mixed bed, with a tall Dracaena, for a centre and surrounded by

Caster-oil and variegated Maples, and edged with the drooping Begonia ascotensis, is the first object that arrests the eye; the groundwork of the bed is composed of Iresine Lindeni, kept dwarf, and edged with Cineraria maritime. Perhaps the great feature of the bed is the rich effect of the Begonia ascotensis, which has a future before it, either for summer bedding or as a decorative plant for the show-house or conservatory.

The elaborate balustrade which circled the formal gardens at Witley Court: - courtesy of the 1938 Sales Catalogue and Worcestershire Archive and Archaeology Service©

The South Portico c.1920:- courtesy of the Lemere (25081-11) – Worcestershire Archive and Archaeology Service©

Fountain and gardens at the height of their magnificence: - courtesy of Ray Jones
(www.surfworcester.co.uk) ©

The next is a carpet-bed with variegated Yucca for a centre, the lines drawn with Golden Feather, and associated with Alternanthera latifolia, the best of the growing kinds, Leucophyton Brownii, and triangles of the yellow Alternanthera magnifica aurea, enclosed by Echeverias, and banded with Veronica repens and Alternanthera amoena, with a double row of Echeverias as an edging. Another pretty arrangement, and one that would give tone to many a large garden, is produced by grouping tall well-proportioned free flowering kinds of Fuchsias, which as seen at Witley are very handsome, having a groundwork of Artemisia judaica, which is in happy contrast to the rich scarlet bells of the Fuchsias – I cannot help repeating, a good way of creating variety and pleasant-to-see old-fashioned plants finding a suitable place, and improved by their association with foliage plants.........'

'Perhaps Mr. Westland had advantages at Witley that are not common elsewhere: the rich verdure of the lawns, the brilliant nature of the surroundings, the situation of the beds nestling at the base of a green bank, and in proximity to sculpture and ornamental vases, all tend to lend attraction to the charming colours and neat designs of the carpet beds. Making allowance, however, for the favourable circumstances enumerated above, there is something still wanting to account for so good a display as Mr. Westland has produced this season.'

An example of the ornate parterre beds at Witley Court with the 'Flora' fountain in the background: - courtesy of the 1938 Sales Catalogue and the Worcestershire Archive and Archaeology Service©

The restored parterre beds in February 2011:- JRH©

One of the Cupids on the restored fountain in 2006:- courtesy of Ashley Horton©

The ruins of the south front of Witley Court in 2006:- courtesy of Ashley Horton©

View of Witley Court: - courtesy of Ashley Horton©

Around the gardens examples of ornate ironwork give a different feature to the various parts of the garden. These were probably made in the ironworks of the Black Country, which the Dudley family owned.

This is an example of the ornate ironwork around the Court Gardens, close to the conservatory: courtesy of the 1938 Sales catalogue and the Worcestershire Archive and Archaeology Service©

On the south front steps pedestals held various interesting sculptures including this fine example of a lion recumbent:

The lions from Witley can today can be found on the *'Lion Terrace'* at Harlaxton Manor now Harlaxton College near Grantham in Lincolnshire.

Harlaxton Manor

Harlaxton Manor was built in the 1830s for Gregory Gregory, a wealthy Nottinghamshire businessman, to replace the original Elizabethan Manor House in Harlaxton Village. Gregory employed Anthony Salvin as the architect for his new mansion. Built in Ancaster stone, it is an exuberant merging of Gothic, Jacobean and Baroque style creating an unforgettable and dramatic impact. There are few houses in England to match the splendid approach to Harlaxton. There is a straight mile long drive across a bridge, under a gatehouse, past *'the pyrotechnic display of the forecourt and gates and screen' (Lincolnshire by Pevsner)* to Salvin's towering facade *'whether by day or night when the building is floodlit, is in itself a memorable experience.'*

Harlaxton College (Manor):- courtesy of Harlaxton College, Lincolnshire©

The lions which stood so proudly on the south facade of Witley Court today are part of the 'Lion Terrace' at Harlaxton College, and still look magnificent in their present setting.

The magnificent lions from Witley Court are part of the 'Lion Terrace' at Harlaxton College: - courtesy of Harlaxton College, Lincolnshire©

On the other pedestals on the South Portico Steps were a pair of bronze lions. The 1938 Catalogue describes as follows:

'A pair of superb Bronze Fighting Lions, a pair of Lions fighting over the body of a boar, two tigers fighting by A. Cain 1878, about 5 ft 6in high and 4ft 9 ins wide, length of 12 ft – full of life and action.'

The lions on their pedestals as seen from the South Portico. In front is the Perseus and Andromeda Fountain and in the distance the view of the Gold gates leading out into the deer park: Courtesy of English Heritage©

The same view over the south terrace in April 2011:- JRH (c)

Auguste Nicholas Cain (1822-1894) -19th Century French Sculptor.

Auguste Nicholas Cain was born in Paris on the 16th November 1822. He was a highly competent member of the '*Animalier*' school. Auguste studied under *Rude, Guionnet and Pierre Jules Mene* whose daughter he married in 1852, which was the tradition of Parisian craftsmen in the mid-19th century. An artisan would marry their mentor's daughter, or even their widow, in order to easily continue the workshop or business. Cain also worked in his father-in-law's foundry, where some of the larger monumental animals were cast, but a few of the larger works were cast by *Barbedienne*. All of his works were exclusively edited by the sculptor himself to a high quality that can be seen in his bronzes.

Cain concentrated a great deal on animals in their natural habitat, especially the gruesome carnivores and combats between animals such as those at *Witley Court*. He sculpted a wide range of domestic and farmyard animals as well, often with a rather humorous touch this creating a personality for each of his creations.

After the sale at Witley Court in 1938 the bronze lions from the south side of Witley were bought and placed on the tall entrance pillars of Harlaxton College in Lincolnshire. They are too high and indistinct to be appreciated which is a pity.

Cain's bronze lions from Witley Court on the entrance pillars at Harlaxton College in Lincolnshire:
- courtesy of Ian Walsh and Harlaxton College©

The Flora Fountain

Nesfield also designed a second fountain to be viewed from the main bedroom apartments. This was the Flora Fountain.

The Flora Fountain as advertised in the 1938 Sale Catalogue: - courtesy of Worcestershire Archive and Archaeology Service©

The 1938 Sales Catalogue makes the following description of this fine sculpture:

'Large circular fountain, about 265 feet in circumference, with a central group of mermen and figures of females holding cornucopia, the whole decorated with dolphins, shells etc., together with the iron and copper main jets within the fountain wall.'

The 'Flora' Fountain in 2011:- JRH© – permission of English Heritage

Detail from the 'Flora Fountain' showing the 'Mermen':- JRH©

In the gardens are examples of different sculpture and vases filled with flowers. One of the finest is the splendid example shown in the 1938 Catalogue with the following description:

'A beautiful French style Garden Bowl ornament on pedestal, decorated with swags and griffins, 5 feet 3inches high, base 3 feet. Square elliptical bowl 4 feet 3 inches by 6 feet.'

Decorated bowl and marble statue of a small child or cherub: courtesy of the 1938 Sales Catalogue and Worcestershire Archive and Archaeology Service©

The Conservatory

The *Journal of Horticulture and Cottage Gardener* of January 2nd 1873 mentions the Conservatory at Witley Court which again gives us a brief insight into what this fine building once contained:

'But before we leave this fine garden we must take a peep into the large conservatory adjoining the mansion, and amidst the groves of Camellia trees we might almost fancy ourselves transported into the flowery land of the East. So healthy, too, with forward bloom-buds, that I anticipated that long before the dark days which precede Christmas the conservatory would have the gay appearance which this plant, in addition to choice Rhododendrons and other plants of a similar character, alone can give. Certainly nothing could look finer, and the whole reflected great credit on Mr. Westland.'

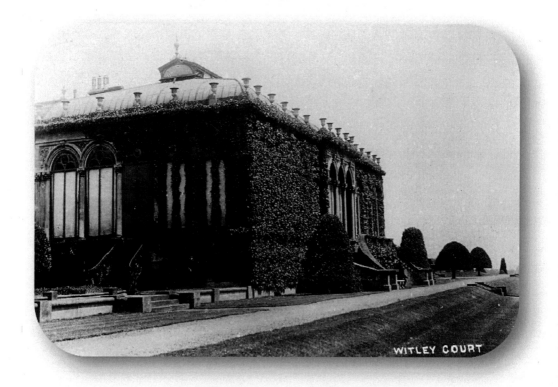

A later picture of the Conservatory or Orangery as it was called covered with ivy. We note the neatly cut bushes and neat lawns: - courtesy of Olive and Bernard Poultney of 'Westwood'©

The October 1851 article from '*The Gardeners' Chronicle*' also mentions the conservatory:

'The conservatory close to the house is a large, spacious structure, in which are noble specimen plants and baskets of grand Petunias suspended from the roof. Camellias planted out and in tubs are in fine health, as are specimen Dicksonias and other New Zealand Ferns. There are also some good palms grouped around the fountain in the centre of the house, and having a noble effect; Dasylirions, Beaucarneas, large Azaleas, and Adiantum Ferns, about 4 feet across, are amongst the most noteworthy plants. The front stage is gay with Campanula pyramidalis and C. alba arranged alternatively with good effect; and the general collection comprises Fuchsias, tuberous-rooted Begonias, Pelargoniums, and the usual run of summer-flowering plants. The back wall is draped with flowering creepers, such as Tacsonias, Coboea scandens variegate, Begonias, and many others.'

A very early c.1860-1900 photograph of the Orangery at Witley Court:- courtesy of Ray Jones©

Close by the conservatory there was a marble figure of a '*Woman and Child*' on a decorative stone base (in stone niche) with an elliptical pool immediately in front:

Marble statue of a Women and Child: courtesy of the 1938 Sales Catalogue and Worcestershire Archive and Archaeology Service©

This splendid marble sculpture when sited in a stone niche, had a pool in front which reflected the statues. This must have had a dramatic effect. The statues can be found today at *Harlaxton College* in Lincolnshire.

This area was known as the Louis XVI Court. Fruit trees were trained up the wall of this sheltered area. Behind the screen wall was the vast coal store. It was said to have been stocked up to 1,500 tonnes, as at peak times the fireplaces, boilers etc., would consume up to 30 tonnes a day. The coal was brought up the River from the *Black Country* to Stourport and then transported by wagon to Witley.

The ruins of the conservatory in 2011:- JRH©

Details from the wall of the conservatory in 2011:- JRH©

The Michelangelo Pavilion

At the end of the curved service wing, the entry into the conservatory was through an elegant pavilion, named the '*Michelangelo Pavilion*' which Daukes the architect designed and based his plans on Michelangelo's Capitoline Museum in Rome in about 1539. The niches were for statues and much of the fine tessellated floor can still be seen in splendid condition today.

The splendid columns inside the Pavilion showing the grooves where thick glass was once fitted directly into the stone itself:-JRH©

The Michelangelo Pavilion and a decorated pilaster from the interior: - JRH©

The Service Wing and the Michelangelo Pavilion in 2011:- JRH©

One of the Tempietto (c. 1900)

There are also fine ornamental pavilions which have been described in the 1938 Sales Catalogue in the following way:

'A small Renaissance Style Domed Tempietto, with Corinthian pilasters and highly ornamental decoration and stone dome, about 12 feet square together with a flight of 7 stone steps with a curved approach.'

The Tempietto in 2011:- JRH©

Decorative details on the Tempietto- JRH@

Some of the kerbstones from Witley Court ended up in the Memorial Gardens in Stourport.

The splendid iron gates at the entrance to the War Memorial Park in Stourport. In the background the once fine bandstand is surrounded by finely carved kerbstones which may have come from Witley Court. The War Memorial Park Gates were made in 1923 by Goodacre, Glover and Butler Limited of Nottingham. The gates are a memorial to the 135 men of Stourport-on – Severn who died serving their country during the First World War 1914-1918. The gates are made of wrought iron and were restored in 1906.

The Fruit Garden

In the copy of the October 1881 '*Gardeners' Chronicle*' there appears a contemporary description of the Fruit Garden:

'The fruit garden is one of the finest sights in the county of Worcestershire. Here are Williams' Bon Chretien Pear propped up by stakes, and Ribsion Pippin, Flower of Kent Apples, the Seckle Pear and Jefferson Plums all needing supports to keep them from breaking to pieces under the crushing weight of fruit, they are bearing. Victoria Plums are also good, but are superseded at Witley by Belgium Purple which never fails and is a fine cooking variety. In the orchard is a fair crop of most kinds has been secured, such kinds as Lord Suffield being abundant and of large size. I should state in passing the Worcester Pearmain does well at Witley, is of good colour and a fair average cropper.

The fine wrought iron gate leading into the Fruit and Kitchen gardens: - courtesy of the 1938 Sale Catalogue and Worcestershire Archive and Archaeolo Service©

Violets are grown in large quantities and Dielytras and such-like ripening off by the hundred for early forcing. The stock of winter-flowering plants are worthy of more than passing notice, not only because of their number, but also because of the great variety of flowers which they have produced at the dullest season of the year. The wealth of winter-flowering plants in cultivation would hardly be believed by many unless an actual example was brought under the notice of those who do not enjoy the privilege and opportunity of gathering information from reliable sources. Mr. Westland pointed out as being particularly useful for autumn-flowering a batch of Aster versicolor in pots, and Veronicas, which he assured me were most useful subjects. Salvias in great variety, including many of those lately sent out by Mr. Cannell, such as Bethlifi Bruanti, Pitcheri and many other varieties, are largely grown. A grand lot of Axaleas, healthy and hard as nails, and a fine batch of Erica melanthera, which are not a showy cut flower, and make a pleasing decorative plant. Tea Roses, scented Geraniums, Hebeclinum ianthinum, Centropogon Lucyanus, Rivina humilis, flowering Begonias, in addition to the commoner kinds of winter-flowering plants, are grown at Witley in large numbers, to meet the increasing demand in cut flowers.

The range of span-roofed pits, formerly employed as fruit-houses, are now being converted into plant houses, and are already stocked with a useful variety of plants. The Witley Pines are not yet forgotten and those interested in that branch of fruit culture and the grand samples of Queens, Charlotte Rothschild, Smooth Cayenne's and others, now ripe or ripening from 5 to 8 lb. in weight, makes one cast a little regret at the fact that Pine growing in England's finest gardens is fast becoming extinct. The houses are each divided into two compartments, and very commodious and convenient plant-houses they make. One house has a fine crop of late Melons, consisting of Eastnor Castle, Sutton's Hero of Bath, William Tillery, and others – a fine crop. The second compartment is filled with sweet-scented flowers Stephanotis, Gardenias, Tabernaemontanas and others, also a batch of Callicarpa purpurea, a useful plan for winter decoration. No. 2 is still occupied with Pines, and the adjoining division with Euphorbias and other well known plants. No. 3 is almost exclusively devoted to Calanthe culture- there are four bulbs in each pot of 9 inches in diameter, such bulbs and leaves are seldom seen! Mr. Westland grows them in turfy loam mixed with cow dung and charcoal. Phaius, Marantas and Dracae, are also grown in variety. Pancratiums, Eucharis and Bouvardias, occupy another division, and a large succession of the latter is planted out-of-doors. Eupatoriums, Lantanas, Habrothamnus, &c., occupy the remaining divisions; and altogether there is fresh evidence at every step you take, that this fine garden is managed by a skilled and painstaking cultivator whose speciality is to leave nothing undone, and to do everything as well as it is possible to do it. W. H.'

The writer in '*The Gardeners' Chronicle* also mentions the examples of trees which were at Witley Court at this time. Much of the woodland and trees in the gardens and the park were later sold off and cut down for their timber value.

'I noticed some fine examples of Conifers on the lawns and slopes adjacent, including Picea Webbiana, Wellingtonia gigantean, over 60 feet high, said to be the finest in England; also a variegated specimen, and a Picea nobilis of unusually large proportions.

CATALOGUE

of approximately

617,915 Cubic Feet

including :—

			c.ft.
3,919	Grand Coppice OAK	containing approximately	248,754
8,338	Other well-grown Park and Coppice Oak	,,	183,430
441	Magnificent ASH	containing approximately	10,649
162	Splendid BEECH	,, ,,	11,436
1,525	SPANISH CHESTNUT	,, ,,	83,497
1,524	LARCH	,, ,,	23,606
131	SYCAMORE	,, ,,	2,941
92	ELM	,, ,,	9,388
2,003	HORSE CHESTNUT, FIR, POPLAR, LIME, WILLOW, etc. Containing approximately		44,214

Together with

15,625 Other SOFTWOODS

now standing marked for sale on the whole of the

Witley Court Estate

conveniently situated for

THE HOME TIMBER TRADE

in close proximity to the industrial centres of England
Birmingham only 23 miles

To be Sold by Auction in Lots at

WITLEY COURT

on

Monday, September 26th, 1938

At 11 o'clock

Auctioneer and Timber Surveyors :—

JACKSON STOPS & STAFF

Timber Department, Estate House, Bridge Street, Northampton
(Tel. 2615/6)
Stops House, Curzon Street, Mayfair, W.1. (Tel. Gros. 1811/4)
Leeds   Cirencester.   Edinburgh   Dublin.

'The next feature of interest (and not the least interesting either), are the dells which afford a very enjoyable retreat from the more classic grounds. From the north side of the garden a brook flows and forms a succession of pools a mile in length. This deep valley is effectively planted with American plants and ornamental trees and shrubs, with a profusion of spring flowering bulbs and plants.'

One of the pools from Witley Court: courtesy of the 1938 Sales Catalogue and the Worcestershire Archive and Archaeology Service©

The boathouse on the front pool in 2011: - JRH©

This rustic boathouse can also be seen on the front lake: - JRH©

The Golden Gates

At the far end of the formal gardens on the East side of the Court enclosed by a stone balustrade are the splendid gates, which were exhibited at the Paris Exhibition of 1862.

The magnificent gates which came from the Paris Exhibition of 1862:- courtesy of the 1938 Sales Catalogue and the Worcestershire Archive and Archaeology Service©

From this point the cricket ground could be seen to the east with the park containing a herd of deer making a beautiful sight for the visitor. An archery green and a nine hole golf course completed the picture. Here also is the historical Oak tree which has been measured at 38 feet in diameter; from here you could have viewed the five lakes all within a radius of a mile. Today all this fine parkland has reverted back to rich farmland.

Herd of Red and Fallow Deer at Charlecote Park similar to those which once roamed the park at Witley Court: - JRH© (see colour plate)

The Berrow's Worcester Journal from 28th June 1873 gives another extract from the *Gardeners' Chronicle* which was from the previous Saturday; it again gives an interesting insight into the Witley Court gardens in their heyday:

'On the eastern side of the gardens a water or rill that flows from the hills forms a succession of pools in a deep valley backed by woods. These have a fine effect, and this wooded bank, with the brook flowing on forever at its base, offers grand facilities for other styles of gardening. It would furnish a grand site for American plants by the thousand, wild and semi wild plants and spring flowers by the million – rockeries, ferneries, waterfalls, and, indeed, every natural, rustic, and picturesque mode of displaying the beauties of Nature, and of Art also, veiled under Nature. I should like to see Mr. Westland fairly at work upon this site, exercising his known powers in this direction. The Kitchen garden as it is, and is to be, lies to the west. It is not as it was, for most of the old houses are pulled down, and the new ones are not yet built. Mr. Westland does not wait in patience; and meanwhile, in a few nice half-span houses, and numbers of tumble-down places, he grows a charming lot of plants for the furnishing of his noble conservatory and the immense flower garden, while he grows pines under difficulties, with a success only possible to the greatest masters of the art. Witley Court, as it is, is something like a sportsman in the field with a double-barrelled rifle, one barrel of which persistently hangs fire. The first

shot, the flower garden, has been done with great execution in the fields of Art; and if the second is equally effective in its bag, as there is every reason to believe that it will be, in the direction of practical horticulture – fruits, plants, and vegetable growing, - then will Witley assuredly become one of the most distinguishable, as it is already one of the most beautiful gardens in the kingdom; nay, I rather think a third shot, more effective, perhaps than either of these two, will be heard by the rill, resounding through the dell and over the pools, and reverberating along the whole course of the wooded hill leading to the nursery, where the site is so charming and the climate so good for coniferous plants that a noble picea grandis of pyramidal form measuring 25 yards round the tips of the branches at the base line. One can but wish that the munificent proprietor may soon discharge his second and third shots, and that Mr. Westland may be privileged to add to or gather the spoil, and to see Witley finished on a scale which shall be in keeping with its grandeur and magnificence. Mr. D. T. Fish 'Gardeners' Chronicle –

The Sales Catalogue of 1938, just 65 years after the above article was written, gives some details of what is left of this magnificent Kitchen garden, after the death of the Duchess of Dudley in 1920 and the sale of the Court.

Lot 5

Area about 8 Acres 3 Roods 37 Poles

The valuable Kitchen Gardens and Orchards

Together with

Comfortable Gardener's House, Greenhouses and Outbuildings

The House

Is built of stone or brick, stucco faced, with slated roof, contains:-

On the First Floor – DRAWING ROOM with bay window, **SITTING ROOM, KITCHEN, SCULLERY** fitted with sink and copper, entrance by a secondary door to two offices.

On the First Floor – THREE BEDROOMS, DRESSING ROOM, BATHROOM fitted Bath (h & c).

Adjoining is a fine range of buildings comprising Apple Rooms fitted with racks, Potting Shed, W.C., Basement fitted with two boilers.

The Garden House in 2011

The Greenhouses and Vineries

Comprise:

Five-span Heated Greenhouse. Vinery and Tomato Houses. Two Lean-to Greenhouses

Large range of Brick Built Frames, several of which are heated. Gardener's Boffy, Tool Shed.

Potting Shed and Fruit Room.

The Gardens

Are enclosed with stone and iron railings, and comprise the productive Vegetable Garden in a high state of cultivation. The central gardens are enclosed by a fine brick wall.

The Orchards

Are exceptionally good, having an extremely fine variety of choice fruit trees.

There is a charming topiary Garden in which is a sundial. A Garden Bell is also fixed.

Sheltered Hard and Grass Tennis Courts, complete with surrounds as fixed.

The Kitchen Garden Wall in 2011:- JRH©

The Kitchen garden wall and some of the topiary from 'My Lady's Garden' with the beautiful flower beds alongside this walk: - courtesy of English Heritage©

The openings in the garden wall and a curious metal gate leading to the Gardener's House- 2011:- JRH©

'My Lady's Garden'

To the west of the more formal gardens, Rachel Countess of Dudley, the wife of the 2nd Earl created her own private garden. She was interested in topiary and included examples of those she had seen in the surrounding villages. Locals recalled that she would stop and buy what she liked.

'The examples of topiary from 'My Lady's Garden' and a picture taken soon after the Countess Rachel's tragic death in 1920:- courtesy of Ray Jones© - www.surfworcester.co.uk

During World War One with so many of the gardeners and other male staff away fighting, many of whom would never return, the women tended the gardens as best they could.

The Countess of Dudley's Garden showing the splendid dovecote and topiary, Rachel so loved:- courtesy of Ray Jones© - www.surfworcester.co.uk

'Our Lady's Walk' part of Rachel, Countess of Dudley's favourite garden:-courtesy of Ray Jones©

They did not have the many years of training and apprenticeship of the thirty or so gardeners who once worked at Witley Court.

The site of 'My Lady's Garden' in 2011:- JRH©

The Icehouses:

Close by the Church and the kitchen gardens were the two icehouses, in which before the invention of refrigerators would be stored layers of ice which would provide wonderful cold desserts to the Court. Here were stored all kinds of foods which would be preserved in the cooler temperatures. There were storehouses below the Court itself which were also cool for storage. In 1819 the architect John Papworth wrote:

'The icehouse forms an excellent larder for the preservation of every kind of food liable to be injured by heat in summer; this fish, game, poultry, butter etc., may be kept for a considerable time, indeed in London they were used for such purposes by persons, who deal largely in either fish or venison; and for the table, where coolness is desirable, the use of ice in summer is a great luxury.'

The Icehouses at Witley Court in 2011:- JRH©

The Park

The park at Witley Court was originally laid out in the time of the Foleys and the care and attention to this part of the estate was continued by the Dudleys themselves.

In 1814 *F. C. Laid* has quoted a marvellous description of the park at this time before the Dudleys took over the estate:

'*a venerable avenue directs the view to the house surrounded by luxuriant woods and plantations... the oak is very extensive and its scenery picturesque; the ancient avenues have an air of grandeur beyond the trim lawns of today...*'

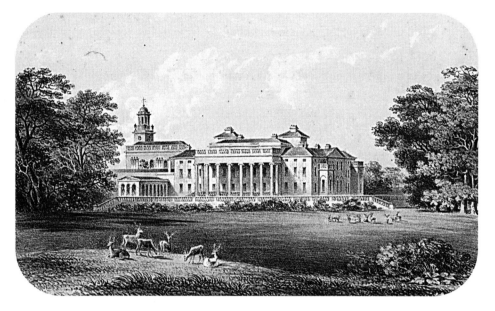

An early view of Witley Court showing the Court situated in the picturesque park which at one time is said to have covered almost 400 acres of prime and ancient woodland:- (ref: BB87/10413) - courtesy of the Worcestershire Archive and Archaeology Service©

In 1848 after the arrival at the Court of the Dudleys *John Noake* gives us a further insight into the fine park: '*there are sheets of water, and islands and cascades tumbling and foaming and undulating surfaces embosomed in evergreens, and labyrinthine paths winding their crooked courses among verdant shrubberies....*'

The Dudleys maintained and cared for the parkland and its many ancient trees. They employed at one time up to six foresters, with each new coppice being identified with a metal plaque which displayed the date of planting and was embossed with the Dudley insignia.

It was a sorry sight to find after the sale of 1938 and after the Dudleys had left the estate that virtually all the 'gigantic ancient oaks' were felled in the sale of standing timber, leaving a mass of tree stumps and debris to be cleared before the land could be used for other purposes such as farming. It was a sad period in the Court's history that trees of over 400 or more years of age were just felled for cash.

The Keeper's Lodge (also known as Deer Park House)

There were several buildings situated within the park itself with the 'Keeper's Lodge' being one of the most interesting.

The Keeper's Lodge from a watercolour by E. F. Burney (1760-1848) – designed by Henry Flitcroft (1697-1769) before 1762. Demolished c.1950.

The lodge was a small replica of the Court itself and strategically situated to overlook the deer park. It was used as a shooting lodge where the many shooting parties at the estate could be entertained. It was sometimes referred to as the '*Dower House*' which suggests that it was a sort of retreat for a senior lady member of the family, such as Lady Georgina when she was widowed or as a retreat for the members of the family or Lady Rachel who may have wished to have some time and seclusion away from the bustle and activity of the Court itself. It would have been exceedingly difficult to find a place where you were not always being observed.

Other buildings associated with the estate would have been situated in the park and away from the main house. These would have included the Engine House which housed a gigantic saw mill and carpenter's shop.

The engine itself, with a flywheel some nine feet in diameter was driven by steam generated by two massive coal fired boilers measuring twenty feet long and five feet tall. These titanic engines could generate up to forty horsepower and the main purpose of this machine was to drive water from the nearby Hundred Pool through pipes to a reservoir situated on higher ground near Martley. From the reservoir here the Poseidon and Flora Fountains could be served. When fully operational they would require up to ten thousand gallons of water, but only for short periods- rather like the fountains at Versailles for Louis X1V which after a fine display of a few minutes took so much water that they would need to be turned off to recuperate the water loss in the reservoir itself.

Chapter Four - The Church of St Michael and All Angels – Witley Court

St Michael and All Angels Church at Witley Court: - JRH (c)

Although physically attached to the Court itself, the church is the responsibility of the Parochial Church Council rather than English Heritage who run the Court. The church is funded and run by the local community. The community began a restoration in 1965 to save this unique building and between 1993 and 1994 the whole of the interior including the splendid Bellucci panels was cleaned. The effect of this restoration is that visitors find both a stunningly beautiful and completely unexpected view when they enter the church itself.

The present church replaced an earlier 13th Century church that had originally stood a little further west than the present one. The first Lord Foley planned the new church, which would become the private chapel of his fine mansion.

The present church was in fact constructed after Lord Foley's death, and paid for by his widow. The architect may have been *James Gibbs* as there are no reliable sources to confirm this. The new church was built with a brick exterior which would have matched the mansion alongside-the interior would have been presumably fairly plain.

The view shows how the new church became part of the main mansion: - JRH (c)

All this was to dramatically change when the second Lord Foley transformed the interior when he bought some of the fine fittings from the recently demolished chapel of the Duke of Chandos's mansion at Canons, Edgware in Middlesex.

Duke of Chandos's mansion at Canons, Edgware in Middlesex

This was one of the finest and most dramatic Baroque interiors of the day and was originally designed by James Gibbs who was employed by Lord Foley to transfer the splendid interior from Canons to Witley incorporating the magnificent ceiling panels painted by *Antonio Bellucci* and ten windows painted by the London glass painter *Joshua Price*, after the designs by *Francesco Slater*.

Gibbs provided a design for an elaborate new vaulted ceiling, constructed not with the usual plaster but in papier mâché at the time a recent invention and having the advantage of being not just malleable but also light. The work at Witley was carried out by *Thomas Bromwich* of Ludgate Hill, London who was probably also responsible for some of the Rococo embellishments in the church.

The triumph of the magnificent ceiling is the central oval displaying Bellucci's painting of the Ascension and the smaller panels of cherubs with the symbols of the passion, while Price's windows depict scenes from the life of Christ.

In the transepts on either side of the high altar can be seen the Foley monuments. The fine pediment tablet to Thomas Foley I who died in 1677, was saved from the previous medieval church, while to the right is the magnificent pyramidal composition commemorating the first Lord Foley and his family.

Memorial tablet to Thomas Foley who owned Witley Court-1655-77. This monument was one of only three items remaining from the original 13th Century Church:-JRH©

The fine large Foley monument was designed in 1753 by Michael Rysbrack (1694-1770) who as one of the leading sculptors of his time. His incised signature can be found on the base of the monument. At the time the cost of the monument was £2,000 which today would have been in the region of c.£200,000.

Details from the Foley Memorial carved by Michael Rysbrack and reputed to be the tallest funeral monument in the country. The mother is shown holding her baby daughter Anna who died at only eight days:-JRH©

The pulpit and font were designed and sculpted by the two Forsyth brothers, William and James, who had been brought down from Ednam in Roxburghshire by Lord Dudley to work on Witley Court.

The splendid carved font by James Forsyth showing angels and surmounted by St John the Baptist: - JRH© (See colour plate).

Detail of the carved marble bowl and angels from the font: - JRH (c)

James usually concentrated on marble sculpture while William chose woodcarving, but they were both talented in both and so it is often hard to genuinely be sure which of the brothers actually carved what, as again James sometimes signed William's work and vice versa.

These oak carved baroque style pews are all slightly different and were supplied by Hindley & Son of Oxford Street in London:-JRH©

The baroque pulpit was designed and carved by William Forsyth and displays four carved panels depicting:- The Sermon on the Mount, Christ preaching from the Boat, the Charge of the Apostles and St Augustine preaching:-JRH©

The following illustration gives a view of the church during the Foley era. The box pews and other Georgian fittings were given to Fawley church near Henley-on-Thames. Samuel Daukes the architect employed by the Dudleys to encase the mansion in Bath stone were also employed to encase the brick church so that it matched the Court.

View of the Foley Church showing the doorway into the Court for the family and servants. Here also is the old pulpit with its sounding board above: - courtesy of the late Bill Pardoe©

In 1913 the fine altar mosaics were added by Salviati and Company and paid for by Rachel, Countess of Dudley. This replaced the original wooden panels which had displayed the Lord's Prayer, the Creed and the Ten Commandments.

View of the Church c.1905:-courtesy of the late Bill Pardoe©

The splendid High Altar mosaic by Salviati & Co. placed here by Rachel Countess of Dudley c.1913:- JRH (c).

The splendid organ in Witley Church, which is said to have been played by Handel himself:-JRH©

Two of the three sanctuary lamps which were a gift from Lady Rachel Dudley, as a thanksgiving offering for the safe return of her husband and his brothers from the Boer War.

Chapter Five - The Time of the 2ⁿᵈ Earl of Dudley

The Right Hon. the Earl of Dudley, P.C.

The 'Worcestershire Lives-c.1899' gives a very flowery description of the 2nd Earl and his career, which shows an interesting insight into his character and interests:

'Few noblemen and country gentlemen there are who are not at the head of every movement started for the public weal. They preside at our meetings. They subscribe to our societies. They support our public institutions. They patronise our charities. Their wives and daughters are the Ladies bountiful in a thousand districts. Their sons go forth to fight our battles by sea and land, while they themselves-

'Mould a mighty State's decrees,

And shape the whisper of the Throne.'

Some such reflections are those suggested by the career of William Humble Ward, Earl of Dudley, Viscount Ednam, of Ednam in the County of Roxburgh and Baron Ward of Birmingham. Although only seven-and-twenty, Earl Dudley has already made a reputation in Parliament, and in the country. His opportunity came with the introduction into the House of Lords of the Employers' Liability Bill. He ardently championed the principle of 'Contracting Out'.

'......The kindest relations exist between the House of Ward and the people of the pit-pierced, forge-lit Black Country. The natives may be rough and rugged, with limbs and faces like the old Bersaerkers, but they have generous hearts. When a few years ago the Earl of Dudley reached his majority there burst forth at Himley and Wordsley, Brierley Hill and Dudley, the most fervid demonstration of attachment and devotion to the Ward family.

'.....A ball given by the Countess on a scale of lavish splendour, the guests comprising the rank and wealth and fashion of the district for miles around.'

'His lordship has seen something of foreign travel. He has been in regions where the Southern Cross lights up the midnight heavens. He has visited the Brazilian Oven, as Rio de Janeiro is not aptly termed, and has gazed upon the fantastic outlines of the Sugar Loaf and on the vermilion roofed city.'

The Right Hon. the Earl of Dudley, P.C. - : courtesy of 'Worcestershire Lives' & the Worcestershire Archive and Archaeology Service©

Lord Dudley and his family are immensely popular in and around the Black Country. His late father distinguished himself by his generous benefactions, notably his princely contributions to the restoration of Worcester Cathedral; while the present Earl's mother possesses personal graces which, in the case of the Princess of Wales, age has not withered nor robbed of their charm.

The present Earl's wife is also a general favourite in society.'

The 2nd Earl of Dudley with his wife the Countess Rachel Anne Gurney:- courtesy of Dudley Archives©

The son of the second Earl had an equally distinguished career, the third generation of the family to carry out outstanding duties in the service of their country. The *'Who's Who in Worcestershire'* for 1935 records the following:

'Dudley, the Earl of (William Humble Eric Ward), M.C., J.P., T.D., D.L. Himley Hall, Dudley, Worcestershire.

Himley Hall, seat of the Dudley Family

Born 1894, London. Son of the late 2nd Earl of Dudley.

Educated Eton, and Christ Church, Oxford.

Married 1914, Rosemary Millicent, daughter of the late Duke of Sutherland.

M.P., Hornsey Borough (Con), 1921-24, and Wednesbury, 1931-32; Parliamentary Private Secretary to Under Secretary of State for India (Early Winterton, P.C.); 1921-23. President Society of British Gas Industries. 1926-27; High Sheriff of Worcestershire, 1930; Chairman of Earl Dudley's Round Oak Works Ltd., and Baggeridge Colliery, Ltd.

Served European War, 1914-18 (M.C., Wounded, Chevalier Legion of Honour).

Heir – William Humble David Ward (1920), Viscount Ednam.'

The Berrow's Worcester Journal of 2nd July 1932 announced the death of the Earl of Dudley. The obituary gives us a very informed account of the 2nd Earl of Dudley's incredible life, a life which spanned the last part of the Victorian Age into the Edwardian and the early 20th Century.

'Death of the Earl of Dudley – Great Services to the State- His Worcestershire Interests.

The death took place in a London nursing home early on Wednesday evening of the Earl of Dudley, who after lying seriously ill at his residence at Le Touquet for many weeks, was brought to London by aeroplane on the advice of his doctor. He stood the journey well, but the improvement in health that had been hoped for as a result of the change did not materialise. He had been growing weaker each day and his condition took a critical turn on Tuesday.

The Earl of Dudley bore a great name and he carried it worthily. He inherited considerable wealth at an early age, and despite some sporting preoccupations in early life, he soon showed a high sense of the responsibilities of his position, and carried them out with conscientiousness and with extraordinary tact and good feeling when he was placed in high State office, but with an independence of mind and judgement which won respect. In Worcestershire he was better known by the older generation, and chiefly by those who were interested in sport and in the County Yeomanry.

In later years he made few visits to the County, one of the latest in public capacity being when Mr. Stanley Baldwin was made an Honourable Freeman of Kidderminster (of which town Lord Dudley was High Steward). Lord Dudley then attended the banquet following the presentation and made a speech of singular grace and felicity.

Lamed in Early Life

The Earl of Dudley was a member of a family which for generations has held places of power and distinction in the State. The barony of Dudley having being created in 1342. He was born on May 25th 1867. No two lives would be more different than that of the late Lord and his father. While the former for many years devoted himself to politics, his father lived largely for art. To his fostering care the opera at that time owed much and Dudley House was famous for its concerts, at which all the artists of the day appeared.

Dudley House, 100 Park Lane – London: - courtesy of English Heritage©

Lord Dudley's Sitting Room in Dudley House: - courtesy of English Heritage©

The London Season- Dudley House in Park Lane

Increasingly the more important families in England liked to have a London house and especially during the 'London Season' when many prestigious families liked to enjoy each other's company in the City at the same time.

Just before Easter each year servants would arrive in London from the main family seat to prepare the London house for the family arrival.

The London Season was a continuous round of parties and dinners, with visits to the opera, concerts, the theatre and art exhibitions - the Royal Academy was one of the most prestigious exhibitions of the year. Many of these families also enjoyed horse racing and would take their carriages and family to Epsom or Ascot where the Royal Family would also be in attendance. Cricket matches were also enjoyed between such venues as Eton near Windsor or Harrow. The Boat Race between Oxford and Cambridge and the Henley Regatta were other venues where the more important families wished to be seen.

For most families the most important part of the London season was the presentation of the debutantes to the Queen at Court in early May.

The magnificent ballroom at Dudley House: - courtesy of English Heritage©

The Picture Gallery at Dudley House: courtesy of English Heritage©

The conservatory at Dudley House: - courtesy of English Heritage©

On Tuesday 29th March 2011-An article by Mike Pryce appeared in the *Worcester News*:

'A Worcester company is a vital cog in the wheel of one of the most costly renovation projects ever carried out to a private house in London.

The property at 100 Park Lane, once the town house of the Earls of Dudley of Witley Court, had a guide price of £42 million five years ago, targeting buyers at 'the top of the billionaire market.'

It has been bought for a knock-down £37.4 million by the Emir of Qatar, who is spending more than £10 million turning it into a family home. Plans include up to 17 bedrooms, a 50 ft ballroom, 80 ft picture gallery and 14 reception rooms of the the highest standard.

Such work needs constant surveillance and remote data specialists Caption Data Ltd of Brindley Court, Worcester, has been called up to supply 38 'black boxes' to monitor environmental conditions and send text messages or e-mails in case of problems. Called RDL/Nanos, the devices monitor temperature and humidity in the rooms and fluid levels and power in the dehumidifiers. Taking measurements every few minutes, every hour, every day, they report back via a mobile phone network to an internet bureau....

The project is due to be completed by the summer of 2012 and will restore 100 Park Lane – which was bombed in the Blitz and had then been commercial offices for four decades – to the peak of the private market.

In the heart of the Mayfair conservation area with views directly over Hyde Park, the house can trace its origins back to 1736. It was the fourth Earl of Dudley, using his vast wealth from the coal and iron industries, who transformed the property in the mid-1800s, lining the staircase with mirrors in imitation of the Palace of Versailles. Sir John Ward, of the Dudley family and his wife Jean Reid, daughter of the American ambassador, presided over some of the most glittering social occasions in the 1920s and 30s.

The kitchens were among the largest in London – one for the food prepared for the family, another for the servants and another for the servants who served the servants.'

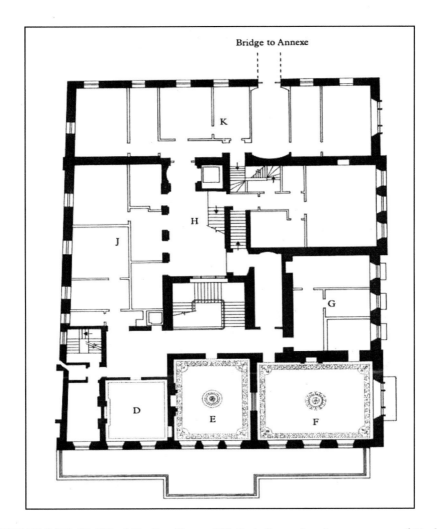

FIRST FLOOR PLAN of Dudley House-100 Park Lane, London:- courtesy of English Heritage©

Key to Ground Floor and the First Floor:

    A.   Waiting Room, former dining room
    B.   Conference Room, formerly light well
    C.   Conference Room, formerly upper part of kitchen
    D.   Former boudoir
    E.   Former blue drawing room
    F.   Former yellow drawing room
    G.   Former red drawing room
    H.   Upper hall, formerly light well
    I.
    J.   Former Ballroom
    K.   Former picture Gallery

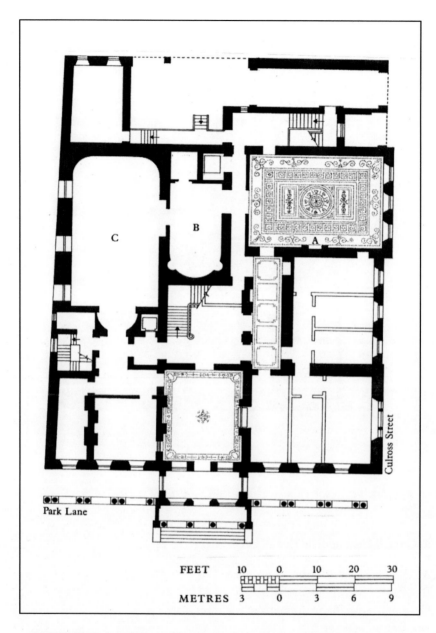

Culross Street

Park Lane

FEET	10	0	10	20	30
METRES	3	0	3	6	9

GROUND FLOOR Plan of Dudley House: - courtesy of English Heritage©

The Dudleys owned another London property at Pall Mall, 7 Carlton Gardens from 1896-1924. Unfortunately this house no longer exists.

As a child of seven or eight the then Viscount Ednam used to be allowed to attend the concerts, and though he was made much of by the prima donna of the time, they did not impress him greatly. Shortly after he went to school at Farnborough, his father fell ill, and that side of his musical life ceased. At Farnborough he lived a pleasant, healthy life, in which a fair amount of work was interspersed with cricket, so that he was well prepared to go to Eton. He entered the house of Mr. Austen Leigh, one of the most famous masters of the time.

During his time at Eton he had the misfortune to hurt his leg while playing cricket, and a short time afterwards he fell down a dark flight of rickety stairs, sustaining a fracture of the thigh bone which lamed him for life. He was laid up for six months, and on returning to Eton, he went to the house of Miss Evans, the last of the 'ladies' who had a house. As Lord Dudley could not play cricket or football he was, as a special favour allowed to ride – a grace only allowed to one other boy, the Duke of Newcastle, and he did for a similar reason. Although he did not have much grip in his lame leg, Lord Dudley nevertheless rode a great deal. He used to hunt with the Windsor Drag, and in later life he took to riding on the flat under National Hunt rules and those of the Jockey Club, while he was also Master of the Worcestershire hunt for many years. At Eton his great friend was the late Lord Hardwicke. In order to get a ride, for Lord Dudley had two ponies, Lord Hardwicke used to dress himself up in Lord Dudley's groom's livery, and in this escaped the notice of the school authorities. After these expeditions, when the two boys were often pursued by irate farmers over whose land they had ridden, Lord Dudley's top boots were always taken away to be cleaned by the groom, and they were shortly afterwards returned to him with a bottle of champagne in each leg. Lord Dudley remained at Eton until he was 17.

The Chapel and Eton College – Windsor©

After leaving school, Lord Dudley went to an Army crammers where he stayed for six months and to France for a similar period, after which he went on a voyage round the world. His travelling companion was Mr, afterwards Canon, Carnegie of Birmingham, one of his closest friends. They started for Brazil, and as soon as they arrived there they found a cablegram stating that Lord Dudley's father had died suddenly, shortly after they had left. Instead of returning home, however, it was deemed advisable that Lord Dudley should continue his travel and a yacht was sent out to him. This was the 'Marchesa', Mr.

Kettlewell's yacht. Lord Dudley sailed to the South Sea Islands, and then to Australia where he remained for six months.'

The 'Marchesa' was designed and built by Lobnitz, Coulborn and Co. in Renfrew in 1877. Registered at 377 tons, she measured 138 and a half feet in length and had a 25 foot beam and was owned for many years by Mr. Charles Kettlewell of Dumbleton Hall, Evesham, and Gloucestershire. Mr. Kettlewell sold the yacht in 1891 and replaced her with a newer steam yacht the 'Queen Marfissa' of 1887, which he renamed 'Marchesa' in honour of her predecessor.

A Formal photographic portrait of William Humble Ward, 12th Baron Ward, 2nd Earl of Dudley and Viscount Ednam: - courtesy of the Dudley Archives©

Early Sporting Achievements

On this boat Lord Dudley travelled for two years, going round the coast of South America, visiting Chile, Peru and Bolivia, and making frequent excursions into the interior. One of these was to Lake Titicaca where he went duck-shooting and in one day got no fewer than 350 ducks to his gun alone. It is an event which is still talked about in the neighbourhood and Lord Dudley became something of a hero in consequence, although he never claimed to be a brilliant shot. From South America he went to visit Lord Carrington, then Governor of New South Wales, and with Lord Loch, who was Governor of Victoria. Mr. Carnegie having returned home earlier, Lord Dudley sent the yacht home and returned on a P. and O. steamer travelling with the late Admiral Sir George Tryon who was then Admiral in command of the station. Some years later one of Lord Dudley's brothers was on-board Sir George Tryon's flagship the Victoria, when she sank, and was one of the few who survived that terrible disaster.

Lord Dudley was not twenty-one when he returned home, and as he could not take his seat in the house of Lords, he went to Cheshire and began to hunt. It was there he met Mr.

'Jock' Trotter, one of the most famous riders to hounds in Ireland, and one of the Masters of the Meath for many years. When Lord Dudley took the Worcestershire hounds, Mr. Trotter became his field master. For the next three years Lord Dudley spent the winter in hunting and the summer in racing. He had a few good horses, among them Fullerton, which had won the City and Suburban and ran second in that race for him.

It was feared by some of his friends that his interest in racing and his taste for gaiety would absorb his energies and interests. But after a period of light-hearted enjoyment he accepted his responsibilities of high social position and great wealth with seriousness. Many believed that his marriage to the beautiful and talented Rachael, younger daughter of Mr. Charles Henry Gurney in 1891, one of the Gurneys of Keswick Hall, Norfolk, gave an impetus to his work. From early youth Miss Gurney had been brought up by her cousin, the Duchess of Bedford, and it was from her house that she was married. The influence of his young wife, full of zeal for the public welfare, made itself felt. Lord Dudley surprised his friends by his energy with which he began to attack his public duties.

Rachael Gurney who became the Countess of Dudley©

His Entry into Public Life

In the early days of his succession to the title he took a great deal of interest in Worcestershire. He stayed occasionally at his magnificent seat at Great Witley, which his father had bought from the Foley family for £900,000 (c. £54,000,000), and had converted at an additional cost of £250,000 (c. £15,000,000) into one of the most palatial residences in the country. He soon got to know his employees on the estate, and when he brought his bride to Witley in 1891 there was great rejoicing. His first venture into public life was as a member of the London County Council, and in 1895 he became Mayor of Dudley, serving for two years, later being elected by the vote of the Council first honorary freeman of the borough. In 1895, the unionists having come into power, Lord Salisbury was pleased to secure so valuable a recruit, and induced him to accept the position of Parliamentary Secretary to the Board of Trade. The Workmen's Compensation Bill afforded him an excellent opportunity of proving his skill in debates and his mastery of detail. He steered the measure through the House of Lords with ability. When war broke out in South Africa, he went out on the Staff of Lord Roberts.

Viceroy of Ireland

On his return in 1902, he was invited by Mr. Balfour to became Lord Lieutenant of Ireland.

This position gave him the opportunity to show his real skills and independence of mind. He had exceptional gifts for the position. He was young and fond of horses, and a keen sportsman. He played golf, motored, shot, sailed and fished, and there were very few sides of the Irish character to which he did not appeal. However, he and Lady Dudley determined that they would make Ireland their home during the whole term of his office. They soon became highly popular with all classes of Irish Society. They not only entertained magnificently at the Castle, they also devoted themselves to making personal acquaintances with the people and their requirements. They took a little house in Connemara and drove about the west of Ireland, making friends with the priests and the peasantry, while Lady Dudley established district nurses in the poorest parts of the country. There were two Royal visits, both memorable in 1903 and 1904. The respect and affection entertained towards them by all classes was shown in a remarkable manner on the occasion of their leaving the position. The streets of Dublin were lined with vast crowds that extended to them the most cordial 'send off.'

View of Dublin Castle

Political Complications

But his reign as Viceroy produced political complications. At this time Mr. George Wyndham was the Chief Secretary, and Sir Anthony MacDonnell was closely identified with the administrative work of that country. In the scheme of land purchase, Lord Dudley absorbed himself. But the Land Purchase Bill having been put through parliament, the Lord Lieutenant appears to have committed himself to a project of devolution that had the support of Sir Anthony MacDonnell and Lord Dunraven, and which led to the resignation of Mr. Wyndham. It was said that Lord Dudley also tendered his resignation to Mr. Balfour. Whether he did or did not, he retained office until the closing days of 1905, when the Unionist Ministry fell. The Earl's labours on behalf of Ireland did not terminate with his tenure of office at Dublin Castle. During the two succeeding years he was Chairman of the Royal Commission on Congestion in Ireland, in which position his intimate knowledge of the conditions of the poor in that country proved of great value. Lord Dudley's views concerning the government of Ireland were far from commending themselves to the Unionist quarter. He went to Ireland a Tory of the Tories but in material matters he was regarded as having weakened, and that modification of opinion was considered to be emphatically confirmed by a speech he made in the House of Lords in the early years of 1906 condemnatory of coercive measures.

In 1908, although a member of the Opposition, Lord Dudley was appointed Governor General of Australia, where he remained until 1911. His genial disposition, love of open air life, and complete absence of assumption, rendered him popular among all classes.

Interest in the Worcestershire Yeomanry

One of Lord Dudley's chief attachments to Worcestershire lay in the County Yeomanry. His father had done much to advance it and it had a troop known as 'Dudley Grey'. To increase the popularity of the troops, he built a riding school in Dudley. In many ways subsequently, when he became commanding officer, he assisted the regiment with liberal gifts, and provided riding schools at other centres in the County. He joined the regiment as an officer soon after he came of age in 1888, and in 1893 attained the rank of major. When the late Earl Roberts proceeded to South Africa at the close of 1899 to take up the command-in-chief of the forces against the Boers, Lord Dudley joined his staff as Deputy Assistant Adjutant-in-General of Imperial Yeomanry. He was one of five brothers who served in that war. From February to May 1900, he took part in operations in the Orange Free State on the British advance on Bloemfontein. On the advance into the Transvaal during May and June of the same year he took part in action near Johannesburg, Pretoria and Diamond Hill and subsequently to the east of Pretoria and at Belfast. He was given the rank of Honorary Major in the Army in October 1900 and had became Lieutenant Colonel of the Worcestershire Hussars on November 10th 1913. When the war broke out the Regiment offered itself for Foreign Service, and in April 1915 it left this country under his command to take part in the Mediterranean expedition. During the training preliminary to their departure Lord Dudley gave substantial sums for providing horses and equipment for the members of the Regiment. He relinquished command of the Yeomanry in 1916 to join the Headquarters Staff of the Fortieth Division.

William Humble Ward, 12th Baron Ward, 2nd Earl of Dudley and Viscount
Ednam, (second from right) with his three brothers – the Honourable John Ward
(far left), the honourable Gerald Ward (second from the left), and the late
Honourable Reginald Ward (far right). They are all in army uniform which
suggests at the time this photograph was taken, they would have been involved
in the Great War (1914-1918):- courtesy of the Dudley Archives (c)

Retirement from Public Life

*After the Great War, Lord Dudley retired from active participation in public and
business affairs, and a private company – Himley Estates Ltd- was formed to administer
the family estates under the general direction of Viscount Ednam. The formation of the
company was marked by the introduction of a helpful policy of development throughout
the Black Country, considerable sites being sold for housing purposes. The Earl of*

Dudley's Round Oak Works Ltd., and the Earl of Dudley's Baggeridge Colliery Company Ltd., were reconstructed.

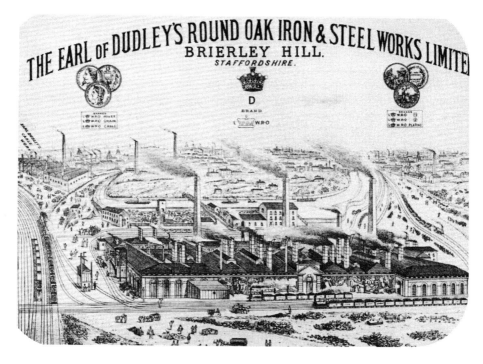

The Round Oak Works Ltd in c.1890 (c)

In 1920 Lord Dudley sold Witley Court to Sir Herbert Smith and in the same year he suffered a 'grievous loss' in the death of his Countess who was accidentally drowned while bathing near Screebe Lodge, in Northern Ireland, which had been purchased by Earl Dudley during his Viceroyalty. The house lies on Camus Bay- a wild and rock-bound inlet, one cove of which runs up into the garden..........

In 1924 Lord Dudley married Mrs. Lionel Monckton, who was better known as Miss Girtie Millar, the actress and retired to his villa at La Touquet, where they became the leaders of the social life of the English colony......

A Wealthy Peer

Lord Dudley at one time ranked among the wealthiest of British peers. He owned about 30,000 acres – rich in minerals –in the heart of the Black Country and at Baggeridge, Sedgley, and had estates in Jamaica. He also owned large ironworks. His father left apart from land a personal fortune of £1,026,000 (c. £61,560,000), which gave a portion of £180,000 (c. £10,800,000) to his younger sons and provided a dowry for Lady Edith Ward, who subsequently became Lady Wolverton. The income of the settled estate was charged with £7,000 a year for his widow, Georgina Countess of Dudley who was assisted in the management of her property by the Earl of Wharncliffe and there were other charges that reduced the bulk of the revenue handed over to the Earl on his attaining his majority. His mineral estates were estimated to yield about £120,000 (c. £7,200,000) a year. He was at one time the patron of thirteen livings including Old Swinford; Kidderminster; Shelsey Beauchamp; Holt; Great Witley, St. John's Stourbridge; St. Thomas's Dudley, Himley, Pensnett, Kingswinford, Wordsley and Sedgley, but most of these advowsons have since been sold.

For some time Lord Dudley was Master of the Worcestershire Hounds and to his generous support the Worcestershire Cricket Club largely owed its survival during the critical years 1913-15.

Lord Dudley was created G.C.V.O in 1903, G.C.M.G. in 1908 and G.C.B in 1911.

Lord Dudley always took a kindly interest in affairs in the City. He gave generously to the fund for the creation of the Victoria Institute, he was elected President of the Worcester School of Art in succession to his father, he presided at a dinner given by the Worcester Rowing Club and on his marriage the Club presented him with a cider cup.

The Victoria Institute in Worcester: - courtesy of the Worcestershire Archive and Archaeology Service©

He was succeeded by his eldest son, Viscount Ednam, Unionist member for Wednesbury, who was born in 1894, was educated at Eton and Christ Church, served in the War, in which he was wounded and received the M.C. and the Legion of Honour, and was member for Hornsey from 1921 to 1924. Lady Ednam sister of the Duke of Sutherland was killed to the lasting grief of her innumerable friends in the Meopham air disaster in July 1930. She left two young sons. Lord Dudley leaves three other sons and three *daughters. Viscount Ednam's elevation will cause a by-election in Wednesbury, where he won by a majority of 4,156.*

The funeral will take place at the family burial ground at Himley Hall at 2.30 p.m. on Saturday, and a memorial service will be held at St. Margaret's Westminster at 11.30 a.m., on the same day. Arrangements are being made for a special saloon on the 11.30 a.m. train from Euston to Dudley Port, returning to London on the 4.28 p.m. train from Dudley Port.

The Meopham Air Disaster

The Meopham Air Disaster occurred on 21st July 1930 when a Junkers F13ge from Le Touquet to Croydon with two crew and four passengers crashed near Meopham, Kent with the loss of all on-board. The report of the inquiry into the accident was made public. It was the first time in the United Kingdom that an accident report had been published for public viewing.

A Junkers F13ge similar to the one involved in the disaster

The plane was owned by the pilot Lieutenant Colonel George Henderson who had loaned his aircraft to Walcot Air Line to operate a charter flight between Le Touquet in France and Croydon Airport just south of London. As the aircraft was above Kent, it appeared to disintegrate. All the passengers except the pilot fell from the aircraft and ended up in an orchard. All of them perished.

The passengers included Frederick Hamilton- Blackwood, 3rd Marquis of Dufferin and Ava a former soldier and politician, and Viscountess Ednam the wife of the Viscount

Ednam and sister to the Duke of Sutherland. The other passengers were Sir Edward Ward and Mrs Sigrid Loeffler.'

Lady Rachel Dudley (1867-1920)

The Times of June 28ᵗʰ 1920 wrote a memoir which reads as follows:

'Rachel Countess of Dudley was the younger daughter of Mr. Charles Henry Gurney, a member of the Norfolk Family of Gurney, of Keswick Hall. Her mother was Alice, daughter of Mr. Toby Henry Prinsep, a distinguished Anglo-Indian official, still remembered by the survivors of the artistic and musical society of London in the 'sixties and seventies'. Another daughter of Mr. Prinsep married Earl Somers, and her daughter, Lady Adeline, became Marchioness of Tavistock and subsequently Duchess of Bedford. From early girlhood Miss Rachel Gurney was brought up by this cousin, who died last April. It was from Adeline Duchess of Bedford's house that she was married, on

September 14th 1891, to the young Earl of Dudley, King Edward (then Prince of Wales) being present at the wedding.'

Keswick Hall in Norfolk

Chris Cunneen:

'On the 14ᵗʰ September 1891 at Chelsea the Earl of Dudley married Rachel Gurney. She was described by Ada Holman as 'beautiful as a marble statue....a carved lily'. A conservative, Dudley was parliamentary secretary to the Board of Trade in 1895-1902 and in 1902-05 an extravagant and controversial lord lieutenant of Ireland. In 1899 he had served briefly in the South African war. In March 1908, partly at the urging of King Edward VII, Dudley was appointed governor general of Australia, a post which the Liberals had found difficult to fill because of their weakness in the House of Lords and Australia's apparent preference for a rich peer. During her husband's governor general ship Lady Dudley also asserted herself in the public area: and in August 1909 she launched what became Lady Dudley's Bush Nursing Scheme, but the project faltered through lack of funds.

By October 1910 the Dudley's estrangement (they separated in 1912) had virtually become common knowledge; John Norton's 'Truth' charged the earl with 'concupiscent capers'. Other newspapers reported the relations between Dudley and the second Fisher cabinet, which had taken office in April 1911, were strained. Partly this resulted in Labour discontent with the increasing vice-regal allowance. In March 1911, after months of rumours of impending retirement, it was announced for personal reasons, Dudley was returning to England. On 31ˢᵗ July he relinquished office. Deakin wrote of him: 'His ambition was high but his interests were short-lived... he did nothing really important, nothing thoroughly, nothing consistently....he remained...a very ineffective and not very popular figurehead.'

Government House in Sydney New South Wales

During World War 1 Dudley commanded a Yeomanry unit in Egypt and Gallipoli. Lady Dudley also served, setting up a hospital for Australians and clubs for officers in northern France. In 1918 she was appointed C.B.E and was awarded the Royal Red Cross. She drowned on 26ᵗʰ June 1920 while sea-bathing in Ireland. In 1924 Lord Dudley married Gertie Millar, musical comedy actress (the original 'Our Miss Gibbs') and widow of Lionel Monckton. Survived by the four sons and three daughters of his first marriage, Dudley died of cancer in London on 29ᵗʰ June 1932.'

The death of Lady Dudley was first reported in '*The Times*' on June 28ᵗʰ 1920 and again on the 30ᵗʰ of that month. This later account gives the details of the accident:

'*Later details concerning the death of the Countess of Dudley were that she travelled from London on Friday, and went to Galway by the morning mail on Saturday, leaving the train at Recess and driving to Screebe Lodge.*

Screebe Lodge- the Irish home of the Dudley Family

It was an unusually warm afternoon, and she decided to bathe from the little jetty at the back of the lodge. Miss Norman, her maid, accompanied her to the water's edge. Lady Dudley was not an expert swimmer, but was very fond of bathing and could swim moderately. Miss Norman watched her take a lifebelt and plunge into the water. She swam about 30 yards from the jetty, still holding on to the lifebelt.

After remaining for some time in the water, Lady Dudley suddenly seemed to struggle, threw up her hands, and sank without a moment's warning. The maid screamed for help, and the caretaker at Screebe Lodge at once put out in a boat. Assisted by some men working in the grounds, he succeeded in recovering the body within a very few minutes, but there was no sign of life. Dr. Kennedy O'Brian, who arrived soon afterwards, attributed death to heart failure.

Lord Dudley arrived yesterday from Worcestershire after a somewhat difficult journey. Crossing from Holyhead on Monday night, he took the morning mail to Dublin to Galway, but the train was held up at Athenry Junction, 14 miles from Galway, because the railwaymen refused to continue the journey when armed policemen entered the train. Lord Dudley succeeded in getting a motor car and by this means covered the remaining 50 miles of his journey. Lord Ednam, Lady Dudley's eldest son, is serving as a captain in the 10th Hussars at Tully, County Clare, and he reached Screebe by motor car on Sunday.

It is the wish of Lord Dudley that Lady Dudley should be buried at the family seat at Witley Court, Worcestershire.'

Lady Dudley left seven children, all of whom survived her. To two of them King Edward stood godfather, to one Queen Alexandra, and to one King George.

COUNTRY LIFE

THE JOURNAL FOR ALL INTERESTED IN COUNTRY LIFE AND COUNTRY PURSUITS **ILLUSTRATED.**

Vol. III.— No. 72. [Registered at the G.P.O. as a Newspaper] *SATURDAY, MAY 21st, 1898.* [Price Sixpence. By Post 6½d.]

The cover of the 'Country Life' – Illustrated for May 21st 1898. Photographer A. Ellis of Upper Baker Street showing Lady Dudley and Children: - courtesy of Country Life©

'*...She was indeed, one of those rare combinations- a woman who joined the deepest domestic affections with wide unselfish sympathies for every kind of suffering. It has been said of her that she had 'a genius for kindness,' concealed it is true under a reserved and even absent manner, but absolutely sincere. With this went a keen intelligence, much* knowledge, and a judgement singularly clear and sane. She read largely, and was equally at home in the 'belles lettres' and in the economic discussions of the day; and in the acquisitions which fortune had bestowed, her instinct was to share with others, and not keep them to herself.

During the war her talents were employed in various ways in the service of the country, and Lady Dudley's name will be gratefully remembered by thousands of officers who passed through the clubs at the bases in Northern France which owed their establishment to her. She became a Commander of the Order of the British Empire in 1918, and was also decorated with the Royal Red Cross.'

On July 3ʳᵈ 1920 'The Times' printed an article relating to the funeral of Lady Dudley:

'The funeral of the Countess of Dudley took place yesterday at Great Witley, Worcestershire, in the presence of a large assembly of friends and tenantry. The body arrived on Thursday from Ireland and was deposited in the chapel in the village. At noon the first part of the burial service was held in the church adjoining Witley Court, and the mourners then proceeded to the place of interment, a piece of ground chosen a few years ago by Lady Dudley, who named it 'The Memory Garden'. The mourners were:

The Earl of Dudley, Viscount and Viscountess Ednam, Lady Honor Ward, Lady Morvyth Ward, the Hon. Roderick Ward, Lady Patricia Ward, the Hon. Edward Ward, the Hon. George Ward, the Hon. Robert Ward, Lady Evelyn Ward, Colonel Gurney, Sir Thomas and Lady Troubridge, Sir Gilbert and Miss Claughton, Colonel Sir Robert Moncrieffe, Colonel J. B. Stracey-Clitherow, Mr. Elliot, F. Barker and Major Z. Cartwright, Mr. G. B. Cartwright and Mr. E. J. Munday representing the Himley tenantry.

Others present were the Earl and Countess Beauchamp, Lord Sandys and Lady Winnington.

On the coffin were placed the nine decorations which had been bestowed on the Countess, and a bunch of Connemara heather, her favourite flower, was dropped by Lord Dudley on the coffin in the grave. The Rev. R. A. Wilson and the Rev. H. G. Monroe conducted the service. The coffin was carried out of the church by 16 workpeople and then was enshrouded in a large Red Cross flag by Lord Dudley, Lord Ednam and the Hon. Roderick Ward.

A memorial service was held yesterday at St. Margaret's Westminster, and was conducted by the rector, Canon Carnegie.

Queen Alexandra was represented by Earl Howe, the Duke of Connaught by Sir Malcolm Murray, Princess Christian by the Hon. Mrs. Evelyn Cecil, and Princess Beatrice by Miss Minnie Cochrane, and there was also a large congregation.'

The Late Countess of Dudley

Wife of the 2nd Earl of Dudley, who was Lord Lieutenant of Ireland, 1902-6, and
Governor General of Australia, 1908-11.
Her Ladyship died on June 26th at Screebe Lodge, Connemara, Ireland.

On the right are three Views of the Private Burial Ground near Witley Court, Worcestershire,
where the interment took place on Friday, July 2nd, 1920.

1. Entrance.
2. Memory Garden, designed by the late Countess.
3. Burial Ground showing the Grave covered with Wreaths. At the head of the Grave is the beautiful Cross
sent by the Countess's Children.

207

The Children of Rachel Gurney and William Humble Ward, 2nd Earl of Dudley

1. *Lady Gladys Honor Ward – b. 1892, d. 5th December 1961.*
2. *William Humble Eric Ward, 3rd Earl of Dudley – b. 20th January 1894, d. 26th December 1969.*
3. *Lady Morvyth Lillian Ward– b.c. 1896, d. 11th March 1959.*
4. *Lt..Col. Hon. Roderick John Ward – b. 13th April 1902, d. 2 October 1952.*
5. *Lady Alexandra Patricia Ward– b. 24th August 1904, d. 7th July 1964.*
6. *G/Capt. Hon. Edward Frederick Ward– b. 20th November 1907, d. 1987.*
7. *George Reginald Ward, 1st and last Viscount Ward of Witley – b. 20th November 1907, d. 15th June 1988.*

Rachel Ward, Countess of Dudley was buried in the 'Memorial Garden' she herself had created. On the four sides of her grave are quotes from Shelley's 'Adonis' – around her are buried some of her children and grandchildren, all at peace and close to the magnificent palace of Witley Court where she spent so much of her life.

St Margaret's Church - Westminster

St Margaret's Church sited alongside Westminster Abbey appears in the story of the Dudleys on several occasions, as well as being mentioned as the church where the memorial service was held for the Countess Rachel after her tragic accident in Ireland.

St Margaret's Church-Westminster:-courtesy of The Dean and Chapter of Westminster Abbey©

In 1065 Edward the Confessor gave orders for the consecration of the abbey church of the Benedictine monastery at Westminster. However, the monks had been disturbed by the ordinary people of Westminster who came to hear Mass. The monks now set about building a small church next to the Abbey. The exclusive church was dedicated to St Margaret of Antioch about whom little is known, though her cult was extremely popular in the Middle Ages.

It seems that St Margaret's church was built in the latter part of the 11th century although there is no precise date. From then until the dissolution of the monasteries by Henry VIIIth, ministry to the increasing population of Westminster was undertaken by the monks of the Abbey. This arrangement was the basis for a very close relationship between St Margaret's church and Westminster Abbey ever since.

The first church was Romanesque in style and survived until the reign of Edward III (1327-77). Its nave was then replaced with one in the Perpendicular style, the chancel still being in good repair at this time. Towards the end of the 15th century, however the whole church was reported to have been in a very poor state and needed almost complete rebuilding. Robert Stowell is said to have been the builder in 1482. This work continued for many years and the rebuilt church was reconsecrated on the 9th April 1523. Despite restorations in the 18th, 19th and 20th centuries, the basic structure remains the same.

St. Margaret's Unique Status

In July 1189, the Abbot and Convent of Westminster received a grant from Pope Clement III which confirmed that St Margaret's Church was outside the jurisdiction of the Bishop of London. In 1222, the Abbey and its property was declared not only to be outside the diocese of London, but also exempt from the authority of the Archbishop of Canterbury.

Then Elizabeth I refounded Westminster Abbey as a collegiate church in 1560. She maintained St Margaret's from episcopal authority and made her new foundation a 'royal peculiar', subject to the authority of the Sovereign as Visitor. St Margaret's church and parish were part of this peculiar jurisdiction until 1840 when they were placed within the diocese of London. By the 1970s the resident population of St Margaret's parish had dwindled to a few hundred and in 1972 'The Westminster Abbey and Saint Margaret Westminster Act' defined the church's status. Its parish was reallocated to neighbouring parishes while the church and churchyard were placed once more under the governance of the Dean and Chapter of Westminster, with one of the Canons of Westminster serving as the Rector of St Margaret's.

Berrow's Worcester Journal

— PICTORIAL SUPPLEMENT. —

Gratis]   SATURDAY, MARCH 7th, 1914.   [Gratis

The Countess of Dudley immediately after looping the loop with Mr. Hamel, and the Witley Court House Party. (Photo: Max Fischer, 10 Barbourne Road, Worcester):- courtesy of Berrow's Worcester Journal©

Spectators at the Worcester Flying Exhibition (Photo: Dowty, Worcester):- courtesy of Berrows's Worcester Journal©

Gustav Hamel: June 25ᵗʰ 1889- missing May 23ʳᵈ 1914

Gustav Hamel was a pioneer British aviator who was educated at Westminster School and learned to fly aged 21 at the Bleriot Flying School at Pau, in Southern France. Gustav gained the Royal Aero Club's Aviator's certificate no. 64 and the Aero-Club de France certificate 358.

Gustav's first flight of note was on the 24ᵗʰ March 1911, when he flew from Hendon to Brooklands in a record 58 minutes.

In one of his famous exploits, he flew a Bleriot on Saturday 9ᵗʰ of September 1911, covering 21 miles between Hendon and Windsor in 10 minutes to deliver the first official airmail to the Postmaster General. Included was a postcard he had written en route.

On 27ᵗʰ July 1912 The Hinkley Times reported:

'Mr Gustav Hamel, the famous aviator, brought his aeroplane to the Outwoods and gave a demonstration of powered flight. This would have been the first time that most Hinkley people had witnessed a motorized aeroplane. The aeroplane flew over Burbage and Sketchley. Many people in Mount Road saw the plane as it flew low over their heads. A mishap at the conclusion of the flight made any further flying that day impossible.'

Disappearance

Just two months after his air display at Worcester when Lady Dudley took to the air as his passenger, Gustav disappeared.

In those early days of flying, this was an dangerous endeavour, and accidents were common. Gustav was to die before he was 30. He disappeared over the English Channel on 23rd May 1914 while returning from Paris in a new 80hp Morane-Saulnier monoplane he had just collected. At this time of the 20th Century there was speculation that he had been a victim of sabotage, but no trace was ever found and the story faded with Gustav's memory.

Chapter Six - Entertaining at Witley Court

One of the most spectacular examples of the entertaining at Witley Court during the Dudley Era was the *Coming of Age* celebrations of the 2nd Earl of Dudley in 1888. *The Berrow's Worcester Journal* of Saturday, August 11th 1888 gives a first-hand description of the events which had taken place at Witley Court the week before:

'THE COMING OF AGE OF THE EARL OF DUDLEY

Rejoicings at Witley

Tuesday Proceedings

The rejoicings at Witley, to celebrate the coming of age of the Earl of Dudley, began on Tuesday. His lordship attained his majority on the 25th May, but for various reasons the festivities proper to so auspicious an event were postponed till the present month.

Witley Court in all its magnificence: - courtesy of Olive and Bernard Poultney of 'Westwood'©

It is rather more than three years since the late Earl died, and his son received the title when he was only 18, being in this respect like his father, who also came to the estates while still a very young man. At the time of his father's death, the present Earl fresh from Eton, had just started on a voyage round the world, accompanied by his uncle, the Hon. R. Moncreiffe, and a tutor, and having visited all the strange and fair places of the earth, he returned to England in May 1887. Since his return he has especially identified himself with the county regiment of Hussars (of which his father was for some years commandant), and is now captain of the Dudley troop. He also takes a lively interest in sport in various forms, and is the possessor not only of a fine stud of hunters, but several race horses. During his minority the Countess of Dudley was guardian of her son, and under the late Earl's will, trustee of the estates, which she has managed with remarkable tact and judgement.

The South Portico designed by John Nash in 2012:-JRH©

Presentation of Addresses

The proceedings on Tuesday began with the presentation of addresses to the Earl. At 12 o' clock the Rev. J. P. Hastings (Rector of Martley) with Mr. J. G. Rogers and Mr. J. Davis attended at Witley Court as a deputation to present to his lordship an address signed by his tenants at Martley, and by other inhabitants to the number of 50, the Earl being Lord of the Manor of Martley.

...........The address, which was illuminated and bound in the form of a book.

The Earl of Dudley in accepting the address said he entertained a very kindly feeling towards the parish of Martley, and valued the expression of their good wishes. He hoped it would be found that he did not take any less interest in his tenants there than the late Earl did.'

At three o'clock a deputation from the Holt estate arrived at Witley Court and the Earl and Countess received them and replied to the given address.

'The address from Holt was a beautiful work of art, and was executed in a manner to make it a permanent memorial of the occasion. The design was at once rich and chaste. The address was within a single border, in the top left hand corner of which was an etching of Holt Castle, and in the lower left-hand corner similar representation of Holt Church. Between the two was the Dudley coat of arms, in their proper honours in a diaper background. At the top and bottom was a foliated border in a running scroll in gold, on a chocolate ground, and on the right-hand was a similar border on a pale blue ground. The address had an inner mount of gold and an outer mount of pale punch grey, and was enclosed in a gold frame having an irregular granulated surface. The whole was enclosed in a rosewood case, lined with crimson velvet and with a plate glass front. Mr. J. C. Gibbs, of the Worcester School of Art, illuminated the address, which was mounted and framed by Mr. Mason.'

Holt Castle and the Dudley Coat of Arms

The main event of these magnificent events was the 'County Ball' which gives us an insight into the entertaining at Witley Court at its most extravagant and most glittering.

The County Ball

'The rejoicing really began with a ball on Tuesday night given at Witley Court to some of the principal personages in the county. The invitations were sent out in the names of the Earl and Countess of Dudley, 'Requesting the pleasure of _____ company on Tuesday, August 7th, to celebrate the coming of age of the Earl of Dudley. Dancing 9.30.' The invitation was printed in gold upon white, with the Dudley monogram and coronet in one corner. Great preparations were made at Witley Court to carry out the plan with as much éclat as possible. To the ballroom itself no preparatory touches were needed, for it is as it stands a monument of decorative construction dazzling in its splendour.

The magnificent ballroom at Witley Court: - courtesy of English Heritage© (see colour plate)

The remains of the magnificent ballroom in 2012:-JRH©

Its dimensions are 110 feet by 56 feet, and it occupies part of the east side of the Court. The striking features of the room are the pair of Corinthian columns, flanked with pilasters of the same order, which stand at each end, the fluted shafts gleaming like marble, and the richly carved capitals blasted with gold. The same characteristics, of elaborate designs in gold upon a pure white background, meet the eye everywhere around the walls and ceiling. The wall on the west side of the room is divided into deep panels with true semi-circular heads, those on the same side as the fireplace being filled with magnificent landscapes, with figures, wrought in tapestry, such as one must go to the Louvre to match, and which from a distance of a few yards cannot be distinguished from oil paintings. The other panels on this side of the room, and all the panels between the windows on the opposite side of the room, are occupied with great mirrors. From the ceiling hung eight crystal candelabra each one holding 30 lights, and for sole ornament there are placed at intervals along the walls alabaster columns supporting vases of the same precious material. The room is upholstered in chocolate and gold. The smoking room, which opens out of the ballroom at the north end, was converted into an ante room and the dining room, opening out of it at the opposite end, was used as a buffet.

Upon the terrace outside the ballroom, a supper tent was erected by Mr. H. Griffiths of Worcester, 60 feet long by 33 feet wide, the roof and the sides being lined with part-coloured canvas, in alternate bands of crimson and white. The floor of the tent was boarded, and it communicated by a covered way with the ballroom, and by another covered way with the corridor leading to the kitchen. The decorations for the supper tables included choice fruits, palms and decorative plants.

For the pleasure of guests who wished to walk in the free air the terrace on the south side of the Court was thrown open, and the darkness relieved by innumerable fairy lamps arranged as borders to the lawns and the steps descending to the terrace. Access was also given to the great conservatory, where amongst the camellias and palms in the centre and the flowering plants along the sides, beamed hundreds more of fairy lamps, and overhead Japanese lanterns contributed their share of brilliant colour and light to the illumination.

Sculpture Gallery and Front Hall at Witley Court: - courtesy of English Heritage©

Within the Court as well as without there was the same manifestation of a desire to study the comfort and taste of guests. The long picture gallery was converted into an extra drawing-room, and besides being furnished as such was the subject of eminently effective floral decoration. In the centre a large 'Seaforthia palm' was placed, with a climbing stephanotis in flower trailed among the branches, and at its base were grouped maiden hair ferns among white spar stone.

In other parts of the gallery were disposed a variety of palms and maiden hair ferns. At the end a billiard table was placed. The two permanent drawing rooms of the Court were thrown into one, which also received a decoration of palms, gloxinias, and other stove flowering plants, ferns, &c.

The Picture Gallery: - courtesy of English Heritage©

The drives from the Stourport and Worcester lodges to the principal entrance to the Court, at which guests were set down, were lighted with hurricane and other lamps, hung at frequent intervals.

The extensive stabling of the Court was utilised to the utmost, and in order that all horses and carriages might be put up on the spot, temporary stalls for nearly 100 horses were erected, with a framework of timber and a canvas roof and back. For the benefit of the servants of guests a super tent, 60 feet by 36, was erected by Mr. H. Griffiths, who we may say, supplied all the tents and tent material used in connection with the festivities.

The number of invitations sent out for the ball was 330, of which 214 accepted. Among the invited guests who had intended to be present was Mr. John J. Jones of Abberley, whose untimely death kept several of his friends and relatives away who had accepted.

Abberley Hall:-courtesy of Jo Roche©

The late Ald. Holland was likewise among those who had accepted the invitation of the Earl and Countess.

The number we have given of course does not include the family and the house party at the court. These were – the Earl and Countess of Dudley, the Hon. John Ward, the Hon. Robert Ward, the Hon. Reginald Ward, the Hon. Cyril Ward, the Hon. Gerald Ward, Lady Edith Ward, the Countess of Coventry, Lady Barbara Coventry, Lady Dorothy Murray, the Hon. Mrs. Ronald Campbell, Master Campbell, Miss Campbell, the Hon. Mrs. Claughton, Mr. Piers Claughton and many more.'

The article includes an extensive list of other guests and also clergy. The laity included many important local families and guests which included:

'The Hon. George Allsopp, M.P., Mr. F. Ames and Mrs. Ames.

Mr. Robert Berkeley, Lady Catherine Berkeley and family, Mr. James Best, Mr. Best, and Mr. H. Best, Mr. J. Brinton and family, Mr. Broome (Areley House) and Mrs. Broome.

Lord and Lady Churchill, Mr. J. H. Crane (High Sheriff of the County) and Mrs. Crane, Mr. H. Caldicott (Mayor of Worcester) and Mrs. Caldicott, Mr. J. R. Cookes, Miss Cookes and party, Captain and Mrs. Childes, Mr. A. C. Cherry and Mrs. Cherry, Colonel Carmichael.....The Hon. R. H. Eden, Mrs. Eden and party, Captain E M.Everitt.

Sir Douglas Galton (Hadzor House), Lady Galton and family, Captain Hubert Galton and Mrs. Galton, Mrs. Cameron Galton and the Misses Galton, Mrs. Cameron Galton, Mr. E. W. Greene, Mrs. Greene and family, Mr. S. Greensill and Mrs. Greensill.

Mr. G. W. Hastings, M. P., and Mrs. Hastings, Mr. E. W. Haywood and the Hon. Mrs. Haywood, Captain Hill, Captain Howard, Mr. G. V. Horyold, Mr. and Mrs. Winsmore Hooper.

Mrs. John Lea and the Misses Lea, Mr. Nowell Lea, Mr. G. E. Martin, Mrs. Martin and family, Colonel Milward and Mrs. Milward, Mr. Corby Manby, Mrs. and Miss Manby, Mr. W. N. Marcy and Mrs. Marcy.

Colonel Norbury, the Hon. Mrs. Norbury and family. Mr. Tempest-Radford and Miss Radford, Colonel Ruxton and Officers of the 29ᵗʰ Regimental Depot, Norton.........

Sir H. F. Vernon and Lady Georgina Vernon (Hanbury Hall and family.....'

Messrs. Synyer and Gilmer's band was engaged for the ball. Dancing was kept up until after three o'clock, and by four o'clock on Wednesday morning all the guests had left the Court.

Wednesday Proceedings – Presentation of Addresses

'On Wednesday there was a further presentation of addresses to the Earl of Dudley. At twelve o'clock a deputation representing the tenants of the Witley part of the Earl's estates arrived at the Court, and were introduced to the Earl and Countess of Dudley by the Hon. R. H. Eden. ....The presentation took place in the long picture gallery where the Countess first received the tenants and chatted with them with great amiability until the arrival of her son, the Earl.

....The address is richly illuminated on vellum, quarto size. On the first page are the arms and coronet of the Earl of Dudley. The binding is Russian leather, gilt sides, with the Earl's coronet and monogram on the outside in the centre. The address is the work of Messrs. Deighton, Worcester.

Lord Dudley, in accepting the address, said: 'from the bottom of my heart I thank you for the very kind words and cordial expressions of good will which you have used in this address and the speech you have just made. I can assure you I shall keep the address as a life-long memento of this happy day. For various reasons I have up to the present not had the pleasure of spending a great portion of my time at Witley, and have not, therefore, perhaps made your acquaintance to such an extent as I should have done; but having been once round the world I do not feel any great inclination to do so again. I hope, therefore, that in each succeeding year we shall become firmer and better friends, if this is possible (Hear, hear). You will doubtless remember in Aesop's fables the story of an old man who, when dying, sent for his son, and told him to bring him some sticks and to break them one after another. When he had done this the old man told him to bring a bundle of sticks, and asked him to break them bound as they were, which he found to be impossible. This, is, I think, a good instance and illustration of the combination and unity that should exist between landlord and tenants; and if we stand together and with our shoulders to the wheel, I see no reason why we should not stave off these bad times. It is always darkest *before the dawn, and there is no reason why these dark years should not be the herald of brighter years to come. I hope it will be so. I hope that in the future we shall be the best of friends and that I shall have the pleasure of riding a good many seven-mile points with you.'*

Lord and Lady Dudley then took an affable leave of the deputation, and invited them to have refreshments before leaving the Court.'

* *

Following on from this deputation, a Mr. John Hemus arrived with an address from the tenants of the Dudley estate at Wichenford and the principal residents of the parish. This deputation was introduced to the Earl and Countess in the long gallery.

Mr. L. P. Thomas, of St. James's Street London, made the next presentation on behalf of the London tradesmen to the Earl and Countess of Dudley. The address was in the form of an illuminated scroll. The deputation also presented the Earl with a gold cigarette box of solid gold, inscribed with the arms and monogram of the Earl of Dudley, and with the words: '*Presented to the Right Hon. The Earl of Dudley by his London tradesmen as a mark of their esteem on the attainment of his majority.*'

The Cottagers' Festival

'Wednesday was set aside as a day of rejoicing for all the cottagers employed on the Worcestershire estates of the Earl of Dudley, extending from Holt to Kidderminster and Bewdley; and on no part of the festivities were greater thought and energy expended, in order that the day might be a memorable one to the very large numbers of persons who are connected with his lordship by the lowly but honourable relationship of labour. For such a festival the weather was a point of supreme importance, and during all this changeful year no day more serenely glorious has been vouchsafed to the dwellers in these Midland regions. It was such a day as one had almost ceased to hope for, filled with sunshine from morning to night, with a cloudless sky, and the air fresh and tranquil as during the loveliest June day.

And what a scene it was upon which the cheerful sun looked at Witley. No one, even the most unobservant stranger, could have passed that way without becoming aware that something remarkable was going forward. In the village of Witley, flags, mottoes and other decorations were displayed in honour of the day. From early morning trains of wagons were to be seen labouring along the Worcester road, laden with all the paraphernalia of a rural fete, specially charted for the use and enjoyment of Lord Dudley's cottager guests, without money and without price. And soon after midday those guests began to pour into the park through the Worcester and Stourport lodges, those from a distance being brought in vehicles and those from the neighbourhood coming on foot.

Photograph date unknown of some of the villagers from Great Witley. They are dressed to celebrate some event: - courtesy of Olive and Bernard Poultney of 'Westwood'©

The arrangements were made so that a view of all the merry making could be obtained from the south front of the Court; while on the other hand the people from their standpoint in the park got a magnificent view of the Court, the gardens, the fountains, the lakes and the wilderness. A few words with regard to the chief features embraced in that striking landscape will not be out of place. One's first feeling could not but be pleased admiration at the marvellous art lavished upon the mansion and its ornamental gardens. Then upon a closer attention one remarked the formal style- Italian in the technical description of it – in which gardens are laid out, the dome-shaped or pyramidal Portugal laurels, golden yews or variegated hollies on this side of the garden being balanced by other shrubs of a like formal cut and of the same species on the opposite side, while the interspaces are relieved with carpet bedding, rhododendrons and other flowering shrubs, and as a background for the whole is the bright green turf of the most perfectly kept lawns conceivable. Towering above the formal cut shrubs to which we have referred are many specimens of conifers of a splendid growth, and serving as a limit to the south are the celebrated gilded gates brought home by the late Earl from the Exhibition of 1862, where they received a prize as a surpassing example of wrought ironwork. Of the wilderness, as offering a contrast to these formal beauties, much might be said – of its unrestrained and partly wild luxuriance, of charming walks beneath Scotch firs and forest trees, by the side of the lake fringed with water lilies, over the rushing cascade, and so till it attains by imperceptible degrees something of the ordered trimness of a more formal style. And so again to the lakes, stretching through the park in long drawn succession from the Hundred pool at the one end, through the Court lake and Worcester lake to Wurbutt's with its island, of which one hears as a kind of 'ultima Thule', so remote as to be discovered only by persons of extraordinary enterprise and daring. And around all, the park, without visible bounds, and in the distance Woodbury Hill, with its singular clump of firs distinguishing it from afar, and Abberley Hill, with its dense woods giving a dark green lustre to the ancient shoulders. Passively regarding such a landscape, or gliding at one's own sweet will through its multiform loveliness, Wordsworth's line came again and again into the mind, 'Earth has not anything to show more fair,' with a new comprehension of the sentiment which led to the most intense poet of nature to apply those words to a scene the majesty of which was dependent upon the evidences of human art.

For those who desire the facts and figures it may be stated that the ornamental gardens cover 6 or 7 acres, that about 10 acres are devoted to the wilderness, and that the combined area of the lakes is about 30 acres. No fewer than 30 persons are employed in the gardens and grounds.

Woodbury Hill close to Witley Court c.1920 showing the clump of fir trees which were planted at the time of the Earl's 'Coming of Age' in 1888:- courtesy of Olive and Bernard Poultney of 'Westwood'©

The initial part of the cottagers' festival was a dinner at two o' clock. In the park, just to the south of the cricket ground, two great tents, 110 feet by 36 feet each, were erected parallel with each other, and without a division between, so that practically they formed one tent. Under these 893 cottagers sat down, and dinner was supplied to them by Messrs. Aldridge (Hundred House), Pitt (Holt), Hundley (Holt Fleet), and Lawson (Martley). Between 40 and 50 tenants of Lord Dudley acted as carvers for the multitude, who received not merely a substantial but in some particulars a choice dinner.

Woodbury Hill from Worcester in November 2012:-JRH©

Lord and Lady Dudley, Lady Coventry, and members of the family and guests at the Court visited the tent during the dinner to see that everything was done for the satisfaction of the guests........After dinner the Earl and Countess of Dudley took up a position in the midst of the company, and after proposing 'the Queen' gave the assembled audience his speech of thanks.

Croome Court- the seat of the Coventry Family: - courtesy of National Trust©

....On dispersing from the tents the cottagers were invited to participate in a great variety of amusements and pastimes, and during the afternoon and evening the Earl of Dudley was unwearyingly in going from point to point to satisfy himself that all the arrangements were working smoothly and pleasantly.

Some distance beyond the dinner tents in the park were merry-go-rounds, swing boats, and a cocoa-nut station, all kept in full operation without charge to those wishing to enjoy them.

The Hundred House at Great Witley which helped supply the food for the celebrations at the Court: - courtesy of Olive and Bernard Poultney of 'Westwood'©

On the lake near the Court a number of pleasure boats were placed, in which those who liked might take a short water trip on the same generous terms. Then under the shadow of some great trees in the park, Signor Somerfield with a troupe of six assistants had a stage where minstrel entertainments, conjuring, a Punch and Judy show, ventriloquism, juggling, and musical eccentricities formed the programme, and during two hours held the eager attention of a large crowd of spectators.

View of one of the lakes at Witley Court: - courtesy of the 1938 Sales Catalogue(ref:728.80942447) & Worcestershire Archive and Archaeology Service©

At four o'clock the fountains began playing and continued for an hour, and as the air was almost motionless and the sun shone full upon the water, they were seen under very favourable conditions. The fountains are among the sights of Witley. They discharge a thousand tons of water in an hour, the central jet of the large fountain rising to a height of 100 feet. The water to supply the fountain is obtained from the cascade in the grounds, whence it is pumped to a reservoir and a pool, formed at the highest point in the park, and discharges itself from the fountains by gravitation.

The spectacular fountains at Witley Court: courtesy of Olive and Bernard Poultney of 'Westwood'©

Between four and five o'clock 416 children from Witley and the neighbouring parishes and 427 women sat down to tea in the two large tents already described, and after tea one of the tents, in which a boarded floor had been laid, was cleared for dancing. The Stourport band played a selection of music......

Simultaneously with the other amusements a series of athletic sports was in progress. First came a 120 yards hurdle race. In the first heat W. Webb was first and A. Dunlop second. In the second heat D. Amphlett and A. Clark ran a dead heat. In the final the winners were W. Webb and A. Dunlop. For the first 120 yards flat race started, W. Woods being first and A. Dunlop second. For the tug of war there were six teams of six men each......

As the day drew to a close, preparations were made for a great display of fireworks, of which the following display of rockets with various colours and effects; ascent of monster balloons with magnesium lights, and a novel description; displays of golden tourbillions, forming cascades of fire in ascent and descent; illumination of the foliage with emerald, crimson, and diamond lights, changing colour continuously; salvo of shells, comprising aerial wheat sheaves torrents and other novel effects; illumination of the fountains, with powerful prisms and ascent of monster balloons; discharge rockets with floating magnesium lights (various); flights of golden tourbillions and rockets, nests of silver and illumination of the foliage; shells and with shell stars; great golden clouds... vast aerial 'feu de joie'. The discharge was by Messrs. Pain, of London, took place in the park close to the south of the Court and provided a successful and highly popular conclusion to the proceedings. The illumination of the grounds had an effect which beggars description by throwing prismatic lights and shields erected around the edge of the four shields and the other tints upon the translucent spray on the gigantic piece of statuary representing Andromeda, which forms the centre illuminated the shrubs by the burning of coloured fire and the final discharge, constituting the 'feu de joie' and more than 300 rockets were used.

Thus ended a day which all concerned seemed bent upon making thoroughly enjoyable and memorable to those who were entertained, while the guests on their part gave themselves up to the festival with an unreserved pleasure not often witnessed in such circumstances.'

Thursday's Proceedings-

Household Address and presentation

'Among the presentations made to Lord Dudley was a very beautiful gift from the household servants at Park Lane, London and Witley. It consisted of a solid silver inkstand, with taper stand, and a pair of silver candlesticks, each article being engraved with the Earl's crest and monogram, while on the underside of the stand were chased the words, 'To the Right Hon. The Earl of Dudley on attaining his majority, from the household servants at Park Lane and Witley Court. May 25th 1888.' Accompanying this gift was an illuminated framed address.'

Dudley House at 100 Park Lane, London in 2012:-JRH©

The Tenants' Ball

As the rejoicings at Witley Court opened with a ball, to which the principal people in the county were invited, so they closed last night with a ball given to the tenants on Lord Dudley's estates at Witley, Kidderminster and Holt. The arrangements were exactly similar to those which have been described in connection with the county ball on Tuesday night. Invitations were sent out to all the tenants, and with a few unavoidable exceptions, they and the members of their families were present. Dancing began at nine o'clock. The total number of guests was 310........'

_____

To-day and to-morrow the Court will play a two days cricket match against the County; and among the matches arranged for next week is one on Tuesday by the Court against Mr. Brinton's team.'

At Witley Court a specially allocated 'square' was maintained for cricket matches. The 2nd Earl was a keen cricketer and many matches were played here at the Court.

In 1895 a nine hole golf course was also laid out in the deer park which hosted many fine and entertaining matches.

Hunting was also part of the social scene at Witley Court with the Worcestershire Hunt meeting at the Court where the hunt kennels were to be found. In the south-west corner of the Deer Park a small enclosure, in the dingle, provided a natural habitat for captured fox cubs which were reared and kept in custody until the end of the shooting season only to be released at various points for the benefit of the hunt. The site was known locally as 'Fox Holes'.

* *

'The Star Hotel Company, Worcester, marked the occasion of the rejoicing at Witley by illuminating the front of the hotel each evening with coloured lamps.'

Star Hotel in Worcester- August 2012:-JRH©

'The rejoicing at Himley and Dudley are fixed for the last week in the month. On the 27th
there will be a county ball at Himley;

Himley Hall the main seat of the Dudley Family: - JRH©

On the 28th a fete for the miners and ironworkers in the Earl's employ, when 3,000 men
will be entertained at Dudley Castle; on the 29th a dinner for the workmen, gardeners, and
keepers at Himley, and amusements in the park there; on the 30th a military tournament in
Himley Park, and a garden party to farm tenants &c. with fireworks at night. The
celebrations on his Lordship's Welsh estates will be held at Llandrillo on the 25th and will
take the form of a dinner for the tenants.

Dudley Castle: courtesy of Olive and Bernard Poultney of 'Westwood'©

The Court was the centre of many family gatherings and celebrations but also the more mundane. The grounds were often open to the public and used by various local groups and charities for their summer fetes and other events.

The Berrow's Worcester Journal of the 19th June 1886 describes such an event, one of many when the local people were allowed inside the park to admire the house, gardens and park of their landlord:

Great Witley

'Whitsuntide – The popularity of Witley Park as a resort of holiday folk at this season was strongly exemplified on Whit Tuesday. During the morning and afternoon a long succession of brakes and other vehicles carried several thousands of persons to this picturesque village. In accordance with annual custom the local club, accompanied by the Stourport Band, paraded through the village and park to the church. After service was over, the procession perambulated the Witley Court gardens, kindly opened by permission of the Countess of Dudley. The magnificent fountains, charming beds of flowers, and sylvan ensemble were a strong attraction with the multitude. Upwards of 3000 people went round the gardens. The gardens always afford a pleasant promenade, but just now they have attained for the season that perfection which is the glory of the skilled gardener. The annual dinner of the club was afterwards held at the Hundred House Hotel, when about 150 sat down under the presidency of the Rev. Canon Melville.

The 'Hundred House':- courtesy of Olive and Bernard Poultney of 'Westwood'©

235

Early view of Great Witley with the Abberley Clock tower in the distance also the Hundred House Coaching Hotel:-courtesy of Olive and Bernard Poultney of 'Westwood'©

Abberley Clock tower on a summer's evening:-JRH©

An unusual back to front image of Witley Court showing the magnificent gardens:-
courtesy of Olive and Bernard Poultney of 'Westwood'©

A good substantial dinner was served up by Mr. Aldridge, the proprietor, in first-class style. The holiday attractions were varied and numerous, and for all there were ample facilities for enjoying the day quietly and pleasantly. On the lawn adjoining the Hundred House dancing and games were vigorously indulged in. There were swing-boats, shooting galleries, shows, &c., in abundance. Others derived a healthful pleasure from strolling through the park. Abberley Hall, more interesting than ever, with its tower and carillon of bells, was also the resort of many.'

* *

Visit of Prince Albert and Princess Alexandra

The Prince and Princess of Wales visited Witley Court on numerous occasions. The Prince, the future King Edward VIIth enjoyed immensely his visits to the Court and the lavish entertainment and shooting activities which were put on in his honour. The Prince enjoyed the opportunity to get away from the formality of official occasions and to enjoy the peace and quiet of Witley set deep in the Worcestershire countryside. Here he could enjoy the lavish dinner parties and entertainment of the wealthy Dudleys without having to leave the estate itself. The sporting facilities included fishing, croquet, archery, hunting, cricket, golf and shooting.

Prince Albert and Princess Alexandra at Witley Court: Courtesy of Royal Worcester Porcelain Archives©

In order from the left to right: Earl Cardigan, countess of Cardigan, Best, Lord Hardwick, Lady Norreys, Lord Arthur Cecil, Hon. Eden, Marchioness of Ripon, Earl of Dudley, Countess of Dudley, Lady Edith, Marquis de Soveral, Prince Albert, the Prince of Wales, Marquis of Ripon, Duchess of Devonshire, Lady Lillian Wemyss, unknown lady, unknown lady, unknown lady, Duke of Devonshire, Lady Hindlip, Sir John Ward, Lady Arthur Cecil, Lord Hindlip and an unknown gentleman.

Detail from the photograph of the shooting party at Witley Court showing from left to right: Marchioness of Ripon, Earl of Dudley, Countess of Dudley, Lady Edith, Marquis de Soveral, The Prince of Wales-Prince Albert, Marquis of Ripon, Duchess of Devonshire, Lady Lillian Wemyss and an unknown lady.

Thousands of pheasants, partridge and other game birds were reared by the gamekeeper and his staff to ensure a good supply of birds, particularly for the shooting season in the autumn.

A 'gun waggon' would follow the guests supplying refreshments when needed. In the morning the gentlemen went shooting and were accompanied by their loaders, with a spare shotgun ready at all times. The ladies would later join the men, but their role was to watch rather than to participate. The ladies would also ensure that the food and drink were ready for the luncheon break and this was often provided in large marquees in the park or close to the Court.

The Berrow's Worcester Journal wrote on one of these splendid shooting parties which took place on a regular basis every year: '....*the shooting party at Great Witley on the visit of the Prince and Princess of Wales had a bag of 1,148 head of game irrespective of the pick-up. There were forty-five beaters and the sport was some of the best ever at Witley.*'

Separate drives for partridge and hares were held in September before the main pheasant shooting season started in October. The culling of the deer in the park was another popular occasion at Witley Court. Provision was made for hides to be constructed, so that the guests could shoot selected deer as they were driven towards them.

The Prince and Princess of Wales at Witley Court with the Earl and Countess of Dudley: - courtesy of Royal Worcester Porcelain©

The coachman and footmen at Witley Court: - (detail) courtesy of Royal Worcester Porcelain Archives©

Mr Walker in his excellent book on Witley Court and Great Witley wrote of a contemporary description of one of the great balls which took place at Witley when the splendid ballroom would have been full of wealthy guests:

'*Precisely at midnight on one occasion when a Ball at the Court was in full swing in honour of Lord Ednam, loud explosions could be heard coming from the Park, causing considerable confusion amongst the assembled guests. Explosive charges had been placed in the stumps of trees which had been felled and the foresters had decided to enliven the proceedings in their own way.*'

'*A ball held in the spring early in the 1900s was disrupted by a sudden and unexpected heavy snowfall. The marquees erected to stable the horses were in danger of collapse and did so, but not before the animals had been taken out. The mud and the slush were such that guests had great difficulty in leaving, so much so that breakfast as well as supper had to be provided.*

This is in contrast to a later tale by which time motor vehicles were becoming available. Another snowfall rendered them quite useless and much to the delight of the horse lovers and the chagrin of the motorists, horses were used to tow the stranded cars and gigs and broughams once more came into their own!!'

* *

One such visit was in 1884 when the Royal couple stayed at Witley with the first Earl of Dudley. There was an official visit to open the Royal Worcester factory museum and on this occasion they were escorted by the Dudleys. The Earl had connections with the Factory as he was a Director and a Shareholder in the *Royal Worcester Porcelain Company.*

The Prince and Princess of Wales with the Dudleys outside the Guildhall in Worcester on their official visit to the City in 1884:- courtesy of Royal Worcester Porcelain Archives©

****

During the 70 years that the Dudleys had owned Witley Court, many fine parties and entertainments would have taken place. Some were for the family and friends others for the local people associated with the Court and the Estate. One example of this can be seen in an article for the *Berrow's Worcester Journal* for the 10th July 1869 when there was a report of a flower show at Witley Court:

'The annual show of the 'Great Witley Floral and Horticultural Association,' which took place on Wednesday, was by the kind permission of the Earl of Dudley, held in a meadow opposite the kitchen gardens, Witley Court. The object of this association, which comprises Great Witley and adjoining parishes, is to encourage the growth of choice flowers, fruits and vegetables, and to create a spirit of emulation among the cottagers, so as

to induce a better cultivation of their gardens. The Earl and Countess of Dudley head the list of subscriptions with handsome donations, and in many other ways contribute to the success which the society has achieved; the gentry and farmers of the neighbourhood are not backward in following the example set them; and the subscription list also contains the names of many persons living at a distance, who thus show in a substantial form their appreciation of the pleasure which a visit to Witley cannot fail to afford.

.....Better weather that that which favoured Wednesday's show could not have been desired. The morning gave promise of a dull day, but during the afternoon the sun broke through the clouds which had overcast the sky, and lent its brilliancy to the charming landscape which surrounds Lord Dudley's palatial residence. The show was opened at two o'clock, and from that hour there were numerous arrivals of visitors. Not a few inhabitants of Worcester, glad to escape for the day from the busy hum of the crowded city to pleasant rural scenes, helped with pleasure-seekers from Tenbury, Kidderminster and other towns to swell the muster of the neighbouring residents who were present in large numbers. That great mark of modern civilisation – the railroad- has not yet disturbed the wonted serenity of the Witley people; therefore the turnpike road and the different vehicles in use thereupon had to be resorted to.

....The whole of the centre stand was occupied by a splendid collection of ferns and tropical plants, contributed by permission of the Earl of Dudley, by Mr. Westland, head gardener. The arrangement was good and the collection was much admired. It comprised some beautiful specimens of Alsophylla, Australis, Alocacia Lowii, Alocacia Gigantia, Alsophylla Ferox, some very good balsams, Blecknum Gibba Montrosa (a new fern raised by Mr. Westland and not yet sent out), Caladium Argyrites, &c.

...Not by any means the least attractive feature of the exhibition was a miniature fountain, which played all the time the show was open. It was constructed by Mr. Beckton, the engineer at the Court and was an excellent example of his taste and skill.

......The Dudley and Worcestershire Band (under the direction of Mr. W. Field, bandmaster) was engaged for the occasion, and their excellent performance of a choice selection of music contributed to the enjoyment of the visitors. Among the selections was the valse, 'Witley Court' composed expressly by Mr. Field. The temptation which the strains of the band held out to the younger portions of the visitors was too great to be resisted, and dancing, after a time been commenced, was continued with spirit for some hours.

.....Attractive as was the show in itself, the occasion was rendered far more attractive by the permission which the noble owner of Witley Court so kindly gave to the visitors to enter his beautiful grounds. Having seen everything that was to be seen in the show tent and listened awhile to the performances of the band, they welcomed the arrival of the hour when they might for a time leave the somewhat crowded enclosure in which the exhibition was located and went their way to the Court. The church, the conservatories, the flower gardens and grounds were thrown open at four o'clock when those who had before the privilege of visiting the Court and those who were entire strangers to it alike eagerly availed *themselves of the opportunity afforded them. They inspected the beautiful interior of the church were conducted through the conservatories, rich in Nature's choicest productions; watched the beautiful fountains at play, and wandered among the skilfully laid-out flower gardens and grounds, which though looking less luxuriant than they did this time last year, gave ample proof of the care bestowed upon them by the talented head gardener.....the only cause for regret being that the Earl of Dudley and his fair countess were not at home to witness the enjoyment which the kindness of the noble earl had conferred.*

At seven o'clock the prizes were distributed to the successful competitors, but the company remained for some time afterwards.' (Thanks to Sue Campbell for finding this article)

The local schools also played a part in many of the events which took place at the Court and particularly at Christmas when the children were entertained and given presents by the Dudley family.

In the early part of the nineteenth century, Dame schools were provided by the local villages which gave the children a rudimentary education. One such school was at 'Holly Cottage' in Great Witley. In 1844 the Dowager Queen Adelaide, who was then living at the Court provided the funds for the building of the first parochial school.

The first village school at Great Witley- funds provided by Queen Adelaide:-JRH©

The new school originally consisted of one classroom with a brick floor and an attached schoolhouse for the teacher. Fees for schooling were one penny a week- the head teacher being paid thirty pounds per annum. When Lord Dudley took over the estate and moved to Witley Court he continued to support the school with expansions to the school as the population grew. Fees rose to four pence a week in 1889 and by 1891 the fees were abolished as education became free to all children. The Elementary Education Act had been passed in 1870 which gave all children the chance of an education. The logbooks at the time give us an insight into what life was like for the children at this time. Epidemics of infectious diseases were common and the school could be closed for lengthy periods. A period of eight and nine weeks was recorded in 1892 and 1893. References to scholarships to '*Oldswinford Hospital School*' under the endowment of *Lord Foley* appear in 1893.

Early photograph of Oldswinford Hospital School

In the September of 1895, a new school building was donated by the second Earl of Dudley on a larger open site opposite the old school. Here were provided much better accommodation and facilities.

The new village school provided by Lord Dudley in 1895:-JRH©

One of the rooms in the new school could be divided with a moveable partition and so a separate room could be used for infants. There were also luxuries such as outside toilets, and an increased playground for the children.

* *

Chapter Seven – *Break-up of the Estate*

The Impact of the two World Wars on the Witley and Holt Estates

The 2nd Earl of Dudley served for many years in the Worcestershire Yeomanry (the Queens' Own Worcestershire Hussars), a volunteer cavalry unit which was first established in 1794 as a result of the disturbances arising from the French Revolution. It was incorporated into the Territorial Force in 1908, later to become the Territorial Army in 1922. During the South African or 'Boer War', the Earl was Deputy Assistant Adjutant to Lord Roberts and it may have been this experience and a sense of premonition which encouraged him, when Colonel of the Regiment, to build up the strength and increase the training in the years prior to the First World War. Training centres were established throughout the county, training personnel in the form of ex-regular soldiers from the Lancers and the Dragoon Guards who were brought in and equipped with horses which were paid for by the Earl and the Estate.

The splendid war memorial to the South African War 1899-1902 – outside Worcester Cathedral:-JRH©

Detail from the Boer War – (1899-1902) memorial outside Worcester Cathedral:-JRH©

The Witley Troop - having had the advantage of local facilities at Witley Court
where the Regimental training camps were also held, were on the rifle range at
Kidderminster when war was declared in 1914. Within 24 hours its members were billeted
at the *Silver Street* barracks in Worcester. In August they were moved to Warwick and
later to Bury St Edmunds, Norwich and Newbury for further training. When at King's
Lynn in early 1915 they experienced war at first hand as the town was bombed by a
zeppelin.

In the April they sailed from Avonmouth to the Middle East to take part in the ill-fated Dardanelles campaign under the Earl as their Colonel, but now as an infantry unit as horses by this time were outdated in modern warfare. In the August of that year Lord Dudley announced that owing to lameness caused by an old injury, he could no longer take command of the regiment in a long dismounted campaign and so was compelled to relinquish his command. The Earl's contribution was considerable and he had established an efficient fighting unit with a high morale which was a significant contribution to the war.

The Dardanelles Campaign - The regiment suffered a larger number of casualties than any other British cavalry unit on all fronts but was throughout, always prepared to respond to anything it was called upon to undertake. The original draft of some five hundred officers, NCOs and other ranks was supplemented throughout the campaign by no fewer than eighteen smaller additional drafts but of the original regiment which had set out in 1915, only three officers and twenty-seven NCOs and men remained to ride into Damascus in 1918. The Regiment finally embarked for England in July 1919 to receive a great welcome from a distinguished company in Worcester on the 6th August.

Lord Ednam also served as Troop Officer with the Hussars and travelled with the regiment to Egypt, but was then posted for staff duties in Europe. Here he was in time awarded both the Military Cross and the French Legion of Honour.

The French Legion of Honour and the Military Cross

The Home Guard

A detachment of the Home Guard was formed in May 1940. This was No. 10 Platoon of C Company of the 11th Worcestershire Battalion; training was mainly carried out at *Abberley Hall* where the Clock Tower provided a vantage 'lookout' point. Duties were shared with the Abberley Platoon and entailed three nights duty each week. The operational role was the manning and covering of a road block at the *Hundred House* hostelry as well as the picketing of approach roads.

The Overall Effect

The effects of the First World War and the Second World War signed the 'death knell' for the estate. Apart from the grief caused by the loss of so many men and boys who went to fight from the Witley Estate, many did not return, so there was the absence of menfolk to work on the estate. There was the influx of evacuees for a time who took their place, and the priority was food production for the war effort. Women played their important role in the land army and in other ways on the estate. The overall effect on the Witley and Holt Estates was profound. The money was no longer available for the maintenance and the running of the estates as previously had been the case – the social, political and economic climate changed dramatically and along with numerous estates after the war many were broken up and sold. This is what happened to Witley.

The Witley Court Sales 1920 & 1925

Sales involving the Great Witley Court and Estate were held in 1920, 1925, 1938, 1946, 1950 and 1954.

In 1920 Witley Court together with its Parkland, associated buildings and adjoining woodlands making a total of eight hundred acres was purchased privately by *Sir Herbert Smith*, a wealthy Kidderminster industrialist. This sale included not just the house but also the contents. The personal belongings and what the Dudleys wanted to keep had already been removed and some of the appurtenances associated with the stable yard. Before the day for the handover a convoy of fourteen horse- drawn carriages of different kinds set off for the Worcester auctioneers.

The remaining eight thousand five hundred acres which made up the vast Great Witley and Holt estates were put up for auction by *'Norbury Smith & Co. of London'* on the Monday and Tuesday of the 27th and 28th September at the Public Hall in Worcester. The one hundred and ninety-two lots were spread over thirteen parishes and included forty-one farms – thirteen of which were in the Great Witley area and nine in the adjoining Little Witley and Hillhampton – several smallholdings, houses and many cottages which had belonged to the farms and which had been used to service the Court. Also in the sale were three licenced houses, the Hundred House with eighty- six acres of land at Witley, the Holt Fleet Hotel and the Red Lion Inn at Holt Heath. Established woodlands were included at the auctioneer's valuations.

The Holt Fleet Hostelry

251

Early print of the Hundred House Inn at Great Witley©

The Hundred House Inn at Great Witley today

Sir Herbert Smith – 1872-1943

Sir Herbert Smith, 1st Baronet (22 June 1872 – 14 July 1943), known as "Piggy" Smith,[iii] was an English carpet manufacturer.

Smith's business was based in Kidderminster. During the First World War he was chairman of the Carpet Trade Rationing Committee and the Man-Power and Protection Committee and was a member of the Board of Control of the Wool and Textile Industries. For these services he was created a baronet in the 1920 Birthday Honours.

From 1921 to 1938 he owned and lived at Witley Court, which partly burned down in 1937 and was never restored. He died at the age of 71 and was succeeded in the baronetcy by his son, also called Herbert.'

Sir Herbert Smith Bt

Sir Herbert Smith was brought up in Kidderminster; he worked initially as a carpet designer and in 1906 when the company he worked for was in financial difficulties - was appointed its general manager. By means of hard business tactics he saw the company once more become prosperous and in 1910 he was in a position to take over the company himself and with other smaller companies created the '*Carpet Trades Limited* in 1920.'

In due course he was made a Baronet for his services to Industry. To celebrate he entertained 1,300 of his employees at Tewkesbury with sports and entertainment in the shadow of the Abbey itself and he also had parties on board six pleasure boats he had specially hired for the occasion.

Said by many to be a hard taskmaster and a ruthless competitor he retired from business a wealthy man in 1922 aged 49. After buying Witley Court he enjoyed travelling and entertaining at Witley Court, although it has been said he only occupied a small part of the immense palace.

Without the vast resources of the Dudleys, Herbert knew he would have to keep his accounts carefully; such an enormous house and grounds needed a great deal of maintenance to keep it up to a high standard. The First World War had seen many local men who had never returned,so there was not the staff anymore to maintain the Court, the gardens and the grounds in their previous immaculate condition.

The staff were reduced, many of the local footpaths were closed to those not associated with the Court, and several of the activities which the Dudleys enjoyed with the local people were curtailed - the old sense of 'family' and 'community' had gone, but the War had also played an enormous part in this situation as well as Herbert himself. The people who had been used to the wealth, privilege and high birth of the Dudleys found it hard to accept their successor who was, they considered, a lowly businessman with 'new wealth'.

Herbert lived at the Court for 17 years and was in fact generous in his support of local institutions including the school and the church, in which he installed electricity along with the Court itself. His friends still recall his generous hospitality and many respected him, but it was a different respect from the adulation and reverence accorded to the more aristocratic predecessors. It was a different age now - the Dudleys and all their wealth and privilege had gone for ever along with many of the other aristocratic families in England.

* *

In 1957 Stanley Fisher the headmaster of the local school wrote about Witley Court in his excellent book *'Collector's Progress'* published by Michael Joseph of 52 Bedford Square, London. Some of his descriptions of the mansion are thought-provoking as by now the Dudleys had sold up the Estate and Witley Court was now not the splendid Victorian Palace it had once been:

'As a young lad I spent many happy days fishing in the great pools a stone's throw from the pillared terraces of such a country mansion. My companion was the son of the estate manager, and when the noble owner was away from home we crept fearfully past the great fountains to peer through the staring, empty windows at the treasures inside. Sometimes we climbed swaying ladders, towering in the darkness, to where beneath a golden dome a great bell terrified us with its sudden clangour as it struck the hour. Beneath, on every side, a petrified forest of chimney-stack, slate and cat-walk. But when the earl was in residence everything was changed indeed! The vast gardens were quickly immaculate under the skilled care of forty pairs of hands, the cavernous corridor in the basement, 10 feet wide and nearly 100 yards long, echoed unceasingly to the quick traffic of countless hurrying, busy feet, and outside, in the sunshine, a roar like thunder and a sudden fierce jet of sparkling, triumphant water, 150 feet in height, paid tribute to the labours of the chief

engineer and his staff in an engine-room from whose tiled floor one could have enjoyed a meal. And every day the fire brigade rehearsed a duty they hoped never to have perform in real earnest, and their master, when the fancy took him, travelled to London by special train.

Such a regime could not last. It so happened that a factory worker from a nearby town was a member of a party that had been invited to visit the lovely grounds, and it is said that as he looked around him at such beauty he said to a companion, 'Someday I will own all this!' His time came. The 1914-18 war gave him his opportunity, which he took with both capable hands. He became a millionaire, and was knighted for his services to industry. So, in due course, one half of his millions was given in exchange for his heart's desire, and the new squire moved in.' – *(Thanks to Jason Fisher for finding this extract for me.)*

The auctions at Witley Court took place after the fire in the September and October of 1938- everything was for sale!

'The auction sale was held in a great marquee, and it was noticeable that the dealers were outnumbered by private buyers from other country houses. There were many strangers, amongst them Mrs. Van der Elst, who sat unmoving, white-faced and clothed in black from head to foot, while her secretary, I suppose he was, bid for piece after piece of graceful, ornate French furniture. What a great deal of brass there was! Scores of saucepans, sets of jelly-moulds, and skillets by the dozen. They went for a song. The Rector bought the first of innumerable over-stuffed arm-chairs for £2 10s 0d., and all the others fetched three or four times as much. And I was so taken by surprise when the bidding on a Georgian chess-table lagged at a sovereign that I lost my chance of a bargain.

What was to be done with these great mansions? The fate of this one, at least, was determined by a careless kitchen-maid who let a pan of fat boil over on the kitchen range. Or so it was said. The collector, at least, can rejoice that he is at liberty to see beautiful and priceless treasures in their proper setting when others are thrown open to the public. The world and his wife can roam the lovely park at Longleat without even having heard of Capability Brown. He can admire its wonderful ceilings and furnishings, and stroll besides its fishponds. He can live for a space in the Golden Age, and – who knows? – he may even realize that there are other things more worthwhile than football pools and the late sports finals.'

Mr Fisher goes on to describe the day he attended one of the sales at Witley Court which makes an interesting and a sad spectacle of what was once the contents of such a gracious and splendid Victorian Palace:

Witley Court in the autumn sunshine of 2011:-JRH©

'Some time ago, more out of curiosity than anything else, we went to a view-day, preparatory to a four day sale. We parked our car in a field, with perhaps a hundred others, at the end of a long shrub-lined drive. The house itself, gracious, seemed to defy the centuries, although of no great age. But just inside the door-as, dispelling all illusion, a gipsy type of dealer sprawled in a Chippendale chair. As a collector I ought to have felt glad that so much furniture and fine china, so many pictures, even a complete staircase, would soon appear on the market, but I could feel nothing but sadness at their imminent dispersal. The following evening the sale was featured on television, the first time, I suppose, such a thing had ever been done. The auctioneers spoke of the difficulty of cataloguing the contents of such a place, and hinted at the excitement of finding, for instance, the remainder of a set of Sheraton chairs in the lumber-room.

......Many pieces at auction are sent to America. Of recent years, since the last war during which many Americans were able to study our way of life and see at first hand the wonders of our heritage of craftsmanship, the flow has been ever-increasing.'

――――――――――――――――――――――――――――

There was a wonderful story of about 100 years ago which gave the following information concerning the wonderful library and book collection at Witley Court:

'A copy of a very rare 'first folio' of Shakespeare's plays has been discovered under curious circumstances, The son of a well-known baronet, delving about the library of the Earl of Dudley at Witley Court came across what he believed to be a first folio. It had been rebound, and one or two pages were missing. It was not at first thought that there was anything in the discovery. The boy, however, had seen a first folio in the British Museum, so he stuck to his guns and eventually the book was sent up to a leading London firm of book dealers. They at once agreed that it was a first folio......'

JACKSON STOPS & STAFF

will Sell the Freehold of

WITLEY COURT

WORCESTER 11 miles   BIRMINGHAM 24 miles

ONCE A ROYAL PALACE

and renowned throughout the world
for its magnificence together with the

WONDERFUL GROUNDS AND PARKLANDS

containing some of the

FINEST STATUARY, GATES, GARDEN HOUSES & EMBELLISHMENTS IN ENGLAND.

Delightful Lakes.   Two Fine Stone-Built Entrance Lodges.

THE HOME FARM

with a Period Homestead and Moat, suitable for conversion into
a Gentlemen's House, and including the historical Woodbury Hill.

Deer Park House, Gardener's House and Enclosed Gardens.

Park and Lakeside Land providing magnificent sites, in some cases
including Houses.————————————Extending to about

1,100 ACRES.

TO BE SOLD AS A WHOLE OR IN FIFTEEN LOTS
(unless previously sold by private treaty), also

THE MAGNIFICENT TIMBER

comprising 617,915 Cubic Feet, mainly mature Oak of some of the
finest quality, and

THE REMAINING CONTENTS OF THE MANSION,

of supreme interest, also probably the finest Collection of **Antique
Rugs and Carpets** in existence. Fine specimens of French and
English Furniture, costly upholstery, Paintings and Decorative
————————————China.————————

THE SALE WILL TAKE PLACE IN THE MARQUEE ON
THE NORTH FRONT OF THE MANSION as follows :—

The Timber and Freehold Estate.	September 26th, 1938, at 11 o'clock.	The Outside Effects	October 4th & 5th, 1938, at 11 o'clock each day.
The Contents of the Mansion and the world famous collection of Carpets and Rugs.	September 27th, 28th, 29th, 30th & October 3rd, at 11 o'clock each day.	The Garden Embellishments in Lots, as a break-up (unless previously sold with the mansion.	October 6th, 1938, at 11 o'clock.

Finely Illustrated Particulars of (1) The Estate and (2) The Contents, with Orders to View—5/- each.
Timber Catalogues, with Orders to View—free on application to the Auctioneers & Surveyors as below :

JACKSON STOPS & STAFF

In 1938 the sale was restricted to the Witley Court Estate and Home Farm. This now totalled one thousand, one hundred acres and included the fire damaged Court together with the contents not affected by the fire. The sale went on for nine days.

That part of the Court which was specified as 'the remaining portion' and 'undamaged' consisted of three floors of the wing nearest the church together with the substantial buildings in the back courtyards and the Conservatory. The former also included servants' and service accommodation on the ground floor, the long gallery and ten principal bedrooms on the first floor, five servants' bedrooms associated with the passageway leading to the church and eight other secondary rooms on the second floor, twenty-four rooms in all. The buildings around the courtyards included the coach house and garages, stables and the loose boxes, harness room and the grooms' room, gunroom, laundry, various workshops as well as a six roomed flat for the stud groom and four other bedrooms for the stable lads or other resident outdoor male staff.

Chapter Eight - The Fire at Witley Court

In 'Collector's Progress' by Stanley Fisher we can get a first-hand description of the fire which was the beginning of the end for Witley Court: courtesy of the Graham Stansfield Collection©

'One night, when my wife and I had been in bed for some hours, we were awakened by loud voices and the noises of cars and motorcycles in the road outside. I got out of bed and looked through the window, to see the sky ablaze with red light. 'The Court's on fire!' I explained, and we dressed quickly, got out my car, and drove along the road to a place from where we had a clear view. True enough, the entire front, the great pillared portico between the two square towers, was studded with squares of orange-red, and as we watched, from the pinnacle tops of the towers themselves streamers of black smoke writhed into the angry sky, to give place, in an instant it seemed, to twisting tongues of yellow flame. And every few minutes, above the roar of the fire, we could hear the thunder of collapsing floors, and see the sudden, swift fountains of sparks shooting up into the sky. Any fire of such magnitude is at once a magnificent and a terrifying sight, but I could think only of the many treasures that were feeding the flames, and we did not stay. Later, we heard that Sir James had been on the South Coast when the news was telephoned to him, and that he had driven through the night in his Rolls at breakneck speed, only to arrive when all that remained of the finest part of his home, the state rooms, was a smoking ruin.

Of course, there had been willing helpers, and a great deal of valuable furniture was saved. One local man cut himself badly by walking straight through a plate-glass window. It was rumoured that there was some looting, and that several fine pairs of silver candlesticks had appeared suddenly on the market. Fortunately, the wonderful church was spared, and only a few weeks ago it was announced that public funds had been granted towards its restoration. As to the rest, the blackened ruins still stand in the centre of the great park, and grass grows on the terraces which were trod by Queen Adelaide and, within living memory, by King Edward VII.

Aerial view of the fire in 1937

Enough furniture had been salvaged to make up a sale which attracted dealers from all over the country, and the view days afforded an opportunity for the villagers to explore what remained of the stately house they had previously only admired from the church drive. They turned out in their Sunday best, as if to pay respect, and for the first time I heard good things said about Sir James. My wife and I walked down the long drive, and took the right fork at the church, to enter what seemed to be the deserted streets of a small town. Stables, workshops, coach-houses, and store-rooms, with here and there a cottage to complete the illusion, until at length we reached the entrance to that great main corridor along which a coach and horses could have been driven and which ended in a tiny semicircle of light far away in the distance.

It was strange to find comfortable living quarters down there in the gloom, the servants'
hall, the housekeeper's room and the butler's pantry, and to see the spacious meat stores,
still-rooms, and pantries which gave mute evidence of a way of life that had gone.

The support of the local people trying desperately to rescue what valuables they could from the
Court as the fire took hold.

Part of the extensive storerooms and service rooms under Witley Court: - courtesy of Jill and Mike Jennings©

The remains of the bell tower, storerooms and the stabling at Witley Court in 2012:-JRH© Thanks to Spencer Trickett for being our most knowledgeable guide on this visit.

The ruins of one of the two towers badly damaged by the fire - the burnt beams can be seen clearly today:-JRH©

Some of the fine 'Carton Pierre' (papier mâché) plasterwork from the State Rooms of the Court still in place some 75 years after the fire:-JRH©

'We mounted a wide stone-flagged staircase and walked along an echoing, dim corridor to the main entrance hall. So far there was no sign of the fire. Then, suddenly, we looked up at the blue sky through a network of charred rafters, and had perforce to pick our way carefully through the blackened debris and shattered glass that littered the once white marble floor. I turned over with my toe a fragment of crimson carpet. I remembered that not so long ago I had crossed that same carpet to the foot of the staircase, and that the butler had glared reprovingly at a servant who had paused from her dusting to watch our passage. The staircase was still there, winding gracefully to the gallery that had once been decked with cabinets of buhl and satinwood, and my eye followed its course to where, high above, a great steel tank, its sides twisted and warped, still rested upon steel girders. All this would not have happened, I thought if Sir James had kept the fire brigade.'

The Picture Gallery at Witley Court- This room was lit by four octagonal dome lights which ran for 21 metres or 70 feet in length with four high east facing windows:- courtesy of English Heritage©

Acknowledgements:

Grateful thanks to the following, who without their continual support and encouragement this project would never have been completed. They are in no particular order, as all have contributed a great deal and without their support this project would never have reached fruition. I have attempted to note all sources and acknowledge copyright and other sources as I have progressed through the book-

English Heritage for giving me permission to look round and take many photographs of the Court and allowing me to use some of their stunning photographs of Witley Court in the past for the book.

To Royal Worcester porcelain for allowing me access to heir archives and for giving me permission to use some of their photographs which were related to the Dudleys and to Witley Court.

Mrs Jane Cox for her continual enthusiasm, encouragement and morale boosting support for this major project. In grateful thanks for performing for me the enormous and time-consuming task of proofreading the manuscripts and giving me useful suggestions on how to improve the script.

Mr Jason Fisher, has again come up with another stunning cover for my book. His design and watercolour of the Court have enhanced the cover a great deal.

Mrs Sue Campbell who every week has found me some more interesting articles, letters, and details of the Witley Court story which have made this book so much more interesting for the reader. Sue has been a great help in always being there to offer encouragement and for finding me useful material and additions for the book.

Worcestershire Archive and Archaeology Service for giving me support and help with my research into Witley Court and permission to use photographs from their collections which have related to Witley Court.

Mr Spencer Tricket from Witley Court who took myself and friends around the Court and gave us the opportunity to see 'behind the scenes,' areas which are not usually accessible to the general public. To thank him also for agreeing to write the 'Foreword' for this book. This is greatly appreciated.

Ray Jones for his splendid photographs which have enhanced the book a great deal- www.surfworcester.co.uk

The staff at Witley Court who have always been helpful and supportive with my research during my various visits.

Mark and Mike Brown from the 'Poseidon Fountain Restoration Society' and other members who made me welcome and encouraged me with my research into the Court.

The staff and helpers whom I have met on my visits to the church of St Michael and All Angels, Great Witley, including Mr Ian Holland and other staff for their support and the Parochial Church Council and parishioners for all their help and encouragement with this project.

The very much appreciated support of the Royal Horticultural Society for allowing me to research their archives and records in relation to Witley Court. The descriptions give an excellent contemporary view of the Court in its heyday.

The author and the printers are grateful to the copyright holders for permission to use quoted materials and images.

The National Portrait Gallery in London.

Every effort has been made to trace copyright holders and obtain their permission for the use of copyright material. The author and the printers will gladly receive information enabling them to rectify any errors or omissions in subsequent editions. All facts are correct at the time of going to print.
